MW00846855

THE ORIGINS OF

THE OTTOMAN EMPIRE

SUNY Series in the Social and Economic History of the Middle East

Donald Quataert, Editor

THE ORIGINS OF
THE OTTOMAN EMPIRE

M. FUAD KÖPRÜLÜ

TRANSLATED AND EDITED BY
GARY LEISER

STATE UNIVERSITY OF NEW YORK PRESS

Published by
State University of New York Press, Albany

Printed in the United States of America

For information, address State University of New York Press, State University Plaza, Albany, N. Y., 12246

Production by Diane Ganeles
Marketing by Dana E. Yanulavich

Library of Congress Cataloging-in-Publication Data
Köprülü, Mehmed Fuad, 1890-1966
[Origines de l'Empire Ottoman. English]
The origins of the Ottoman Empire / by Mehmed Fuad Köprülü; translated and edited by Gary Leiser.
p. cm. — (SUNY series in the social and economic history of the Middle East)
Translation of the Turkish ed. of Les origines de l'Empire Ottoman.
Includes bibliographical references and index.
ISBN 0-7914-0819-1 (CH : acid-free). — ISBN 0-7914-0820-5 (PB : acid-free)
1. Turkey—History—Ottoman Empire, 1288-1918. I. Leiser, Gary, 1946- . II. Title. III. Series.
DR486.K6313 1991
949.61—dc20 90-22723
CIP

10 9 8 7 6 5 4 3 2 1

This Translation is Dedicated to the Memory of
Hüsameddin Güz

A vibrant mind, a generous friend

''*Dostlar beni hatırlasın*''

CONTENTS

ABBREVIATIONS

BSOAS	*Bulletin of the School of Oriental and African Studies*
DOP	*Dumbarton Oaks Papers*
EI^1	*Encyclopaedia of Islam, 1st ed. (Leiden, 1913–42)*
EI^2	*Encyclopaedia of Islam, 2nd ed. (Leiden, 1960–)*
İA	*İslām Ansiklopedisi (Istanbul, 1940–88)*
JA	*Journal Asiatique*
JESHO	*Journal of the Economic and Social History of the Orient*
KCA	*Körösi Csoma-Archivum*
MOG	*Mitteilungen zur Osmanischen Geschichte*
MTM	*Millī Tetebbular Mecmuası*
THİTM	*Türk Hukuk ve İktisat Tarihi Mecmuası*
TM	*Türkiyat Mecmuası*
TOEM	*Tarih-i Osmanī Encümeni Mecmuası*
ZDMG	*Zeitschrift der Deutschen Morgenländischen Gesellschaft*

PREFACE

Mehmed Fuad Köprülü was the most outstanding Turkish scholar and intellectual of the twentieth century. His pioneering work on the history of Turkish literature and Turkish history has had a profound effect on the study of those disciplines in Turkey. Indeed, he is rightly regarded as the father of modern, scientific Turkish research on the culture and history of the Turks. He was born Köprülüzāde Mehmed Fuad on 4 December 1890 in Istanbul. Although related on his father's side to the famous Ottoman Grand Vizir Köprülü Mehmed Pasha (d. 1661), after whom he was named, his family was of rather modest means—his father being a middle-ranking civil servant. He grew up, however, in a very cosmopolitan atmosphere, exposed to different cultural traditions and the intellectual elite of Istanbul and with access to extremely rich library resources.

By the time he was seventeen, Köprülü had decided to specialize in Turkish literature, and he completely immersed himself in that subject. He attended university in Istanbul but never received a degree. In fact, he was essentially self-taught. Between 1912 and 1950, he produced a stream of books, articles, essays, and reviews. These writings included a number of seminal works that won him an international reputation and many accolades. During these years, he also taught at Istanbul University and then Ankara University. In 1943, he left academia and entered Turkish politics. In 1950, he became Minister of Foreign Affairs, a post he held until 1955. The following year, he returned to private life and his scholarly interests. In 1961, he made a short-lived attempt to reenter politics and then retired. He died in Ankara on 28 June 1966 as the result of complications arising from being struck by a vehicle (for details on his life and work, see the introduction to my forthcoming translation of his *Some Observations on the Influence of Byzantine Institutions on Ottoman Institutions*).

Among Köprülü's renowned works is the book presented here, *The Origins of the Ottoman Empire.* Originally presented as a series of lectures delivered at the Sorbonne, it was first published in Paris in 1935 as *Les origines de l'Empire Ottoman.* In this work, the author criticizes Western research on the origins of the Ottoman state, above all H. A. Gibbons' *Foundation of the Ottoman Empire*, for its unscholarly approach; presents for the first time a proper scientific method for studying this topic; and then, using this method, briefly describes the political, social, economic, and religious conditions in Anatolia in the thirteenth and fourteenth centuries that set the stage for the rise of the Ottomans. The last part of the book is basically a synthesis of much of his previous work. *Les origines* was very well received and almost immediately went out of print. It became a kind of minor "classic" and was subsequently cited in virtually all significant works on the history of the Ottoman Empire and many related fields. Although *Les origines* was recently reprinted (Philadelphia, 1978), it is still not readily available. The reissue of this famous book in a major Western language is therefore easily justified, especially in light of the enormous expansion in Islamic, Ottoman, Byzantine, and Balkan studies in the past half century. With this in mind, Köprülü's book is offered here in English in the hope that this will help it return to the hands of interested readers.

The English translation was made from the Turkish edition of this work, which was not published until 1959 under the title *Osmanlı devleti'nin kuruluşu* [The founding of the Ottoman state] (Ankara: Türk Tarih Kurumu) and reprinted in 1984. It was also published under the slightly different title *Osmanlı imparatorluğunun kuruluşu* [The founding of the Ottoman Empire] in 1972 (Ankara: Başnur Matbaası). This edition corrected some of the typographical errors found in that of 1959 and contained a short description of Köprülü's life and personality written by his son, Orhan. Apart from this, all the Turkish editions are identical. It should be mentioned, though, that despite Köprülü's claim that the Turkish and French texts are the same (see his introduction below), this is not entirely correct. The essence of the two works is certainly identical, but there are many sentences and phrases in the Turkish which are not found in the French (cf., e.g., the following pages, Turkish first, 12/17, 13/18, 21/28, 46/55–56, 50/61, 60/73, 74/90). This makes the Turkish text slightly more detailed. And even where the texts fully correspond to each other, there are sometimes different shades of meaning. For example, in the Turkish we find the sentence which begins (p. 29), "Bizantinistler . . . ettiğini söylerler" ("The Byzantinists say that . . . "), whereas the French is (p. 35), "La plupart des byzantinistes estiment que. . . . " Another Turkish sentence states (p. 50), " . . . söylenebilir" ("It could be said that . . . "), while the French is (p. 61), "Il est vrai que. . . . " Furthermore, the paragraphization of the two books is somewhat different and there are a few variations in terminology. For instance, where we find "tribe" in the Turkish, we find "clan" in the French. These differences apparently came about from the fact that the text was originally written in Turkish and was then edited while being translated into French.

The English translation does not include the "note on the author" by Nedim Filipovich found in the Turkish edition. This "note" was Filipovich's introduction to his Serbo-Croation translation of Köprülü's book. The information on the writer and his work given by Filipovich is superseded by that in the introduction to *Some Observations* mentioned above. Köprülü's footnotes have been clarified and recast according to modern usage. Furthermore, sufficient notes have been added to reflect recent research and scholarship on issues raised by the author. A glossary, full bibliography, and map have also been provided. All significant changes or additions to the text and notes, usually for clarification, have been enclosed in braces { }. Köprülü often uses quotation marks for emphasis, paraphrased citations, and other purposes. These have been employed sparingly in the translation. For the transliteration of Turkish, Arabic and Persian words, the system used in the *Cambridge History of Iran* has generally been followed. There are some inconsistencies, however, primarily because words common to all three languages are pronounced differently. As for modern Turkish orthography, ö and ü are the same as in German, c = j, ç = ch, ğ = gh as in Edinburgh, ı = the "o" in atom, and ş = sh.

Finally, this translation benefited from the assistance of several patient friends. Hüsameddin Güz reviewed my work and corrected or improved a number of passages. I am sad to say that he passed away before seeing it appear from the press. Dr. Toni Cross, the Director of the American Research Institute in Turkey, Ankara branch, gave keen editorial advice. Dr. Scott Redford of Georgetown University clarified many of Köprülü's footnotes. Dr. Rudi Lindner of the University of Michigan provided numerous helpful suggestions to update those notes. And my wife Patricia engineered our word processor to accommodate Turkish, as well as Arabic and Persian in transliteration, and frequently saved me from inadvertent crashes—no small achievement.

Gary Leiser

PREFACE TO THE FRENCH EDITION

The creation of a Center for Turkish Studies during the past academic year {1933–34} is, without doubt, a happy and unprecedented event in the history of the Sorbonne. I had the privilege of noting the importance of this event when the Dean of the Faculty of Literature at Istanbul University, Mr. Mehmed Fuad Köprülü, came here himself to dedicate and inaugurate it.

We were sincerely hoping for his visit and assistance. Joining Mr. Albert Gabriel, the Director of the French Institute in Istanbul, scholars and students had organized for a common purpose, namely, to maintain and expand in our country the knowledge of Turkish history, literature, and art in the tradition of a great many illustrious Frenchmen. It was then natural for us to ask an eminent professor at Istanbul University to come in person to provide us with the results of his research, which by no means has been unknown to us, but the merits and results of which we were anxious to ascertain for ourselves.

The lectures that he gave at the Sorbonne have grown in renown and success. Today he has done us the service of publishing them in French, that is, the language in which he recently gave them. And we take this opportunity to thank him for this. Those who heard these lectures will read them with pleasure and genuine profit. Mr. Köprülü has revived a difficult subject. Having available to him all the resources which his knowledge, as detailed as it is comprehensive, of the literature of the subject affords him, he has been able to add (and the people who heard him were struck by this) an exceptional personal erudition and apply to this mass of knowledge his critical talents and his natural appreciation of method.

The explanation that he gave before his audience, and which is found in this book, of the thesis of the historian Herbert Gibbons, and the manner in which he posed the problem of the founding of the Ottoman Empire, which in turn determined the method with which it should be approached, are models of clear, simple criticism. The chapters that follow will give, I believe, the most reliable idea of the political and social situation in Anatolia at the time of the appearance of the Ottomans. As for their ethnic origins, the date of their arrival in Anatolia, and the various phases that mark their transition from an insignificant principality to a powerful state—all of which have long been controversial questions—these issues are all resolved here together in a completely new manner, one which our competent scholars can no doubt debate but which they cannot ignore.

The previous work of Mr. Köprülü, above all his research on Ottoman institutions and the study that he devoted to the influence of Turco-Mongol shamanism on Muslim mystical orders, as well as the critiques he has published of texts, have qualified him better than anyone to study, according to the principles of modern historical criticism, the origins of the Ottoman Empire. It is difficult, however, to present in so few pages a full study of one of the most arduous problems of the history of the medieval Orient.

We are grateful to Mr. Köprülü for having selected the Sorbonne as the place at which to present an explanation and synthesis of the work that has established his reputation, and we hope that he will return to take his place among us and that he will present many times again his scholarly research, and the talent with which he explains it, to the benefit of the French public. It would be with joy and satisfaction that we Turkologists would continue such a collaboration.

Sébastien Charléty

INTRODUCTION TO THE TURKISH EDITION

In 1934, at the opening of the Center for Turkish Studies attached to the University of Paris, I gave three lectures on the subject of the founding of the Ottoman state. These lectures were published in 1935 by the French Institute in Istanbul with a short preface by Professor Sébastien Charléty, who was then rector of the university and a member of the institute, under the title *Les origines de l'Empire Ottoman*. I would like to mention with gratitude the great efforts of my dear friend and old colleague Albert Gabriel, who was at that time the director of the French Institute in Istanbul and a professor in the Faculty of Literature of Istanbul University, to establish this center at the Sorbonne and publish my lectures. While mentioning this old and loyal friend who today {1959} is a retired honorary professor of the Collège de France and a member of the French Institute and is still continuing his incomparable studies on Turkish art, I cannot help but recall with deep sorrow a great many common friends whom we have lost, above all the late Sébastien Charléty.

My book was very well received in knowledgeable circles. Although it was of interest to a limited number of historians and Orientalists, the edition went out of print in a short time. In the fall of 1938, when I returned to Paris from two congresses at Zurich and Brussels, I bought the last copy remaining in the warehouse of E. de Boccard, which had published the book, and gave it to the famous historian Louis Halphen in order to fulfill a promise I had made to him at the Zurich congress. I learned from the bibliography of the *History of the Seljuks of Asia Minor* {in Russian (Moscow, 1941; Turkish translation, Ankara, n.d., ca. 1988)} published by my old friend, the well-known Russian Turkologist Professor Gordlevsky, that it was translated into Russian and printed lithographically in Moscow. The French work was republished in a regular serialized form in Istanbul between 1937 and 1939 in the daily French newspaper *Stamboul*. A great many parts of it were also cited and published in the French weekly magazine *Ankara*, which appeared about the same time in Ankara. Finally, in 1955, Professor Nedim Filipovich translated my book into Serbo-Croatian at Bosnasaray {i.e., Sarajevo, Yugoslavia}, an old center of Islamic and Turkish studies, and published it with a rather long introduction—full of excessive compliments about the scholarly activities and personality of the author.

It seems that there is almost universal reference to my book in the bibliographies of works written in various languages—above all French—on Turkey. For many years a great many foreign researchers, indeed, a great many scholarly institutions, have asked me for copies because of the great general interest that this work has aroused. But after distributing the few copies in my possession, I had, and continue to have, to answer in the negative.

After the publication of this work, reviews of it by certain well-known scholars appeared in several scientific journals. I would like to mention the observations of the great Sinologist P. Pelliot, who was also famous for his research on Turco-Mongol philology and history, in the journal *T'oung Pao* (32 [1936]) and recall the esteemed memory of this old friend with affection and respect. I first had the honor of meeting this great scholar and discussing many subjects with him in Paris in 1923. We met again during the celebration of the two-hundredth anniversary of the Russian Academy of Sciences in Leningrad in 1925, and at the Congress of Orientalists in Brussels in 1938. I met him for the last time in 1939 when we had lunch in a small private room of a famous restaurant—where the Goncourt brothers {Edmond and Jules, French authors} used to meet and have lunch on certain days—near the Opera in Paris. In those days when the Second World War was beginning, I was in Paris to receive an honorary doctorate from the university during the ceremonies held to open the new academic year at the Sorbonne. This lunch was given by some old friends and colleagues who were professors at the Collège de France and the Sorbonne. Despite the very terrible and gloomy world conditions, the time that I spent around that lunch table with those loyal friends, who were among the greatest authorities in Oriental studies, represents one of the happiest and most unforgetable memories of my life. It was such that I could not help but record this short remembrance before mentioning Pelliot's observations on my little book.

In his short review, the great scholar focused on a number of points in my book that concerned eastern Asia and said that he agreed with them. He then corrected certain matters in which I had erred in some points of detail. For example, I stated that William of Rubruck had passed through Konya in 1255 while going to Karakorum, but this occurred on his return and not while en route. He also wondered if the name of the tribe written as *Yisvut* in my book should not be *Bisvut*, and was right in this regard. I did considerable work on the name of this tribe after the publication of his review and the results confirmed just how correct was my scholar friend, who is one of the greatest specialists in Mongolian. Stressing as important the fact that I considered the Ottoman dynasty to be from the Qayı tribe, which came to Anatolia at the end of the eleventh and the beginning of the twelfth centuries, and that I corrected the old mistake made by a great many Western scholars who believed the word *uc* {i.e., *uj* } was the name of a tribe, Pelliot characterized this little book as "excellent." He naturally dwelt only on those points which concerned his specialization and said that generally the book was a *mise au point* "which collected in one place our limited information on the origins of the Ottomans." This short work was not, however, simply one which collected in one place the existing, limited and insignificant material on this subject. Rather, it was the first synthetic attempt to refute almost completely the old theories about the origins of the Ottoman state, to present new theories that were entirely different from those advanced up to then, and to offer to the scientific world the results of twenty years of research on the economic and social history of the Seljuk state and its religious and mystical movements. The great master of Chinese and Mongol research quite naturally refrained from making any comments on these subjects which were foreign to him.

A second analysis and review of my book appeared in the same year in the *Revue Internationale des Études Balkaniques* published in Belgrade (second year, vols. 1–2, pts. 3–4, pp. 303–05). The writer of this short notice was P. Skok, one of the editors of the journal and a professor at the University of Zagreb. This respected scholar, who was well-known for his studies on Balkan languages, said, with the modesty characteristic of a true scholar, that this work "is an extremely good introduction to understanding the Turkish element in the Balkan languages and for this reason he himself was emboldened to discuss it." In his opinion, the problem of the origins of the Ottoman Empire was of the utmost interest to all Balkanologists, no matter what area of Balkan life in which they were working. Professor Skok briefly described the subject of the work and its results and added that the word *osmanlı* {Ottoman} was used with a certain meaning in Serbo-Croatian, that the family name Avdalovich, which undoubtedly derived from the root *abdāl*, was found among some Orthodox families in Banja Luka and Gacko {both in Yugoslavia} but was not encountered among the Muslim Bosnians. Skok agreed with the idea defended in my book that the Turkish nomads, villagers, and city dwellers who came to the Balkans in the fourteenth century were the heirs to the rich civilization of the Seljuks. Recalling that he had discussed in an article entitled "Restes de la langue turque dans les Balkans" (same journal, vol. 1, p. 592 {*sic*}) the very rich linguistic material of Eastern origin concerning urban life that the Turks had brought to the Balkan languages, he concurred with my view that the historical explanation of this derived from the fact that the Turks were the heirs of Seljuk civilization.

After these descriptions showing how well my little book was received by two very renowned specialists, one in Chinese and Mongol studies and the other in the field of Balkan languages, I cannot help but include the thoughts on this work by a very great historian who has acquired widespread fame not only in France but also in the entire world, namely, Professor Lucien Febvre. A true historian in the widest sense of the term, and an erudite and multifaceted scholar the like of whom is rarely encountered, Febvre, as everyone who has more or less studied history and sociology knows, founded in 1929 the journal *Annales d'Histoire Economique et Sociale* with his esteemed colleague Marc Bloch, who was killed by the Nazis in World War II, and, together with his respected friends in various areas of specialization whom he gathered about him, was in the vanguard of a new and broad understanding of historiography. He was also at the head of the French Encyclopaedia which began to be published on a completely new basis after World War I. The journal, which continued to be published by him and his devoted friends during and after World War II—despite several changes in name—is still concerned with publishing the most recent and advanced ideas in the fields of history and the social sciences. Febvre continued his scholarly activity with unshakable enthusiasm even after passing his seventy-fifth birthday. One characteristic of this great master, who unexpectedly passed away about two years ago {1956}, was to express his opinions and observations quite clearly and sincerely and he made no exceptions even with his closest friends and the most famous people. Therefore, the ideas that Febvre advanced with the eye of a true historian about my little book, even though he did not have a special interest in the subject, were important and valuable. Although it might be considered immodest by some, I cannot hide the fact that even today I feel spiritual pleasure and vigor in briefly citing here a few passages from his one-page analysis.

Febvre said that I grasped the problem of the origins of the Ottoman Empire "generally" and "in its totality" and that I really brought it to light. He stated that I applied strict criticism to the texts, replaced fables with scientific knowledge, pointed out a great many errors and mistaken interpretations in Gibbons' book, and, above all, advanced completely historical opinions instead of traditions based in great measure on tales and legends. He added that I did not hesitate to say "I don't know" with regard to problems that my predecessors did not even know how to present much less solve. He finished with these conclusions: "In short, the author, going considerably beyond the narrative stage of history, has produced a solid, clear and synthetic work. There is no need to go into detail on this short, excellent book. Forceful and straightforward, it shows that Mr. Köprülü is a scholar trained in the rules of textual criticism, an historian having the ability to appreciate good work, a man, in a word, who has an aversion to one-sided explanations, who knows how to correct in the process the mass of errors and confusion which have been recorded with blissful indifference in our basic works. Neither social history nor economic history is forgotten in the explanations that are given to us. We should applaud the fact that Mr. Köprülü has himself quite rightly called for a vigorous effort to apply to the research on medieval Turkish and Muslim history the methods practiced by Western medievalists in their field and to save such a vast part of the history of humanity from archaic and out-of-date traditions" (*Annales d'Histoire Economique et Sociale*, 9 [1937], 100–01).

Febvre understood the concept of history in its widest and truest sense and, in this respect, provided guidance over the years to generations in his courses, lectures, works, the French Encyclopaedia that he directed, and especially in the severe but always objective critiques and analyses that he wrote in the aforesaid famous journal until his death. The observations of Febvre on my little book suffice to show how capably he grasped the nature of a work whose subject was far from his own specialization. A number of respected Orientalists who had been occupied with the problem of the origins of the Ottoman Empire, although good philologists, had not been able to go beyond a narrow and simplistic framework when they dealt with historical subjects because they could not escape from the influence of the mentality of narrative history. They could not escape from simplification. The frequent attempts to explain by a single cause, that is, from one aspect, any historical process which has come into existence under the influence of many different factors is nothing but the neglect of the complexity, that is, the reality of life. As an experienced master of history, Febvre, therefore, immediately understood, even from my little book, my approach to the subject and the principles I followed in my work and was quite right to point out carefully and significantly "that I detested one-sided explanations."

It is clear that researchers who are bound to any one doctrine, according to their own biases, usually fall into this error. Instead of trying to understand and explain historical reality, they are satisfied with using only material that suits their work and subjecting it to interpretations forced by their biases in order to show that their "one-sided explanations" are correct. Throughout my professional life, I have always considered such one-sided explanations that force and distort reality to be contrary and dangerous to a genuine and honest understanding of history. Those who think they can try to examine historical events sociologically and believe they can solve everything with simple one-sided explanations are completely alien to a true study of history; and a small group of *philosophes* who have high hopes of describing and explaining the general evolution of human life under the name of "history of philosophy" can also never be considered historians. Instead of enriching our knowledge of human history and advancing it, they have reached completely subjective and imaginary conclusions and have made arbitrary classifications and comparisons, thus misleading a number of thinkers and researchers. Indeed, they have sent them in the wrong direction. Even though esteemed thinkers like Professor Arnold Toynbee are found among these *philosophes*, one must never confuse them with genuine historians. I would especially like to state here that I completely agree with the extensive and forceful criticism of these philosophers of history that Febvre has made in numerous publications.

I have explained and defended my basic ideas about the founding of the Ottoman state in many studies that I have published since 1913 on Turkish literature. In articles that appeared between 1913 and 1918 in journals like *Bilgi Mecmuası* and *Millī Tetebbular Mecmuası*, I described in detail how the view that the Ottoman state "arose from a tribe of 400 tents," as in Namık Kemal's romantic description, was meaningless and that Ottoman literature was a natural continuation of the literature of the Anatolian Seljuk period, in short, that Turkish history and the history of Turkish culture, from their origins to the present day, had to be studied as a whole in time and place. I also presented certain studies as examples based on these main ideas.[1] In *Türk edebiyatında ilk mutasavvıflar* [Early mystics in Turkish literature], which was published in 1918 {2nd. revised ed., 1966; rpt. Ankara, 1981}, I presented definite, irrefutable proof that the Turkish cultural life that developed in Anatolia in the Seljuk period was very closely bound to the cultural life of Central Asia.[2] In the article "Anadolu'da islāmiyet: {Türk istilāsından sonra Anadolu tarih-i dinisine bir nazar ve bu tarihin menbaları}" [Islam in Anatolia: A review of the religious history of Anatolia after the Turkish invasion and the sources for this history, an English translation by Gary Leiser is forthcoming], which appeared in *{Darülfünün} Edebiyat Fakültesi Mecmuası* in 1922, I also stated that, as long as the geographic regions around Anatolia and the religious currents in the Near Eastern Islamic world were not taken as a whole, it was impossible to understand the religious history of the Anatolian Turks. All my subsequent writings can be considered as additional evidence which was derived from the application of this same approach and these same basic ideas and which, in turn, corroborated their validity and forcefulness.

The little book that was composed of the three lectures that I gave at the Sorbonne thus came into existence as the product of this kind of concept of history. While preparing these lectures, I naturally took advantage of the results of my earlier studies and also made extensive use of my previous unpublished research on a number of issues mentioned in those studies. However, because of the need to confine myself to the narrow framework of three lectures, a great many questions were briefly touched on in passing and only conclusions were given. {The lack of an opportunity to present fully} subjects which had been inadequately known, or mistakenly understood, up to then by the scholarly world was obviously a major shortcoming. In particular, I could have suggested a way to eliminate certain views which by that time had become accepted as more or less common convictions, albeit general and vague, but I had no space to present the evidence in my possession with all its richness and strength. Instead, a great many important points that I could have defended most vigorously are only mentioned in passing, a significant drawback for this short book. {Since this work first appeared,} I have published an article entitled "Osmanlı imparatorluğunun etnik menşei meseleleri" [The problems of the ethnic origin of the Ottoman Empire], *Belleten*, 7 (1943), 219–313, and a second article called "Kay kabilesi hakkında yeni notlar" [New notes on the Qay tribe], *Belleten*, 8 (1944), 421–52, in which I was able to explain and defend extensively, that is, in full detail, one of my contentions, which I had previously discussed in various writings, namely, that "the Ottoman dynasty belonged to the great Qayı tribe of the Oghuz."

Although I dwelt on a number of unanswered questions in this book—which up to now have not received any serious or fundamental study—I singled out this Qayı problem, which I had more or less explained before, for the following main reason: In the work entitled *The Rise of the Ottoman Empire* (Turkish translation by Fahriye Arık [Istanbul, 1947]), which was published three years after my book {London, 1938}, my very old friend and dear colleague, Professor Paul Wittek, insisted on defending his opinion that "the Ottoman dynasty invented the palace tradition of being related to the Qayı in the reign of Murad II," {cf. pp. 9–11}. Moreover, my dear friend and authoritative student of Turkish history, Professor Zeki Validi Togan, did not agree that there was no basis to equating Qay with Qayı. J. Marquart had previously asserted that they were identical, and competent Western scholars had accepted his assertion while I had severly criticized it. Based on new evidence, Togan sought to revive Marquart's old theory. After the publication of my aforesaid articles, Professor W. Eberhard stated that, based on Chinese sources, it was not possible to accept Togan's theory on the Qay, and supported my interpretation ("Kay'lar kabilesi hakkında sinolojik mülāhazalar" [Sinological observations on the tribe of the Qays], *Belleten*, 8 [1944], 567–84). Fahriye Arık also further supported my argument with new and very solid evidence showing that "the Qayı seal was used on Ottoman coinage from the time of Orhan Ghāzī to Mehmed II," in contrast to the view of Wittek who claimed that its use was confined to the coinage of Murad II.[3] Later Faruk Sümer, who attracted attention with his valuable studies on the Oghuz tribes, published an article called "Osmanlı devrinde Anadolu'da Kayılar" ([The Qayıs in Anatolia in the Ottoman period], *Belleten*, 12 [1948], 575–614), in which he made extensive use of archival material to strengthen my position even more. He also presented new and strong evidence to prove that a number of my speculations were in fact correct. Indeed, without being carried away by pathological hypercriticism, I am of the opinion that it is no longer necessary to return to this subject which, as I have explained numerous times, is of extremely little historical significance.

After the French text of my lectures was published in 1935, with the addition of some essential but limited notes, I very naturally thought of immediately publishing the Turkish text among the publications of the Turkish Historical Society {Türk Tarih Kurumu}. I felt it was somewhat odd, however, to offer to the Turkish intellectual world a subject like the origins of the Ottoman Empire, which is of the utmost interest to our national history, in the narrow framework of three lectures. It was necessary to either enrich and expand this topic with the addition of abundant notes, or rewrite the work in detailed fashion within a broad format suitable to the requirements of the subject. I could never decide what I should do. Finally, either my scholarly preoccupations or various difficulties of political life prevented me from doing anything.

As the years passed from 1935 to 1959, scholarly research directly or indirectly related to the origins of the Ottoman Empire has advanced without interruption. There has also been important activity in the fields of Byzantine and Balkan studies, which are very closely related to our political and military history. Important texts and research concerning the Ilkhānid period have appeared. New and fundamental work has been done on the social and economic history of the Near Eastern Islamic world and its many problems. In our country as well, sources long known to the scholarly world concerning the Seljuks of Anatolia, like Ibn Bībī and al-Aqsarāyī, some secretarial handbooks {*münşeat*}, mystical and certain important literary texts, and a number of studies, both significant and insignificant, have been published. I can add to this certain valuable archival material related to the first centuries of the Ottomans. The research on this subject by Western scholars should also not be forgotten (see my study entitled "Anadolu Selçukluları tarihinin yerli kaynakları" [Local sources for the history of the Seljuks of Anatolia, an English translation by Gary Leiser is forthcoming], *Belleten*, 7 [1943], 379–522). Finally, there are the important articles on this subject in the Turkish edition of the *Encyclopaedia of Islam* {1st ed., i.e., *İslām Ansiklopedisi*}. Even to list them all here in the form of the briefest and most general catalogue would be neither possible nor necessary.

In the event, while preparing the Turkish edition of my short French book, after many years, and keeping in mind the considerations that I have enumerated above, I have reached the following conclusion: This Turkish edition will appear without the slightest revision in the original form as it was written in 1934, that is, it will be no different from the French edition. Turkish translations of the prefaces to the French and Serbo-Croatian editions will be added and the index of the French edition will be thoroughly expanded to make the work easier to use. Thus today my decision has been realized and the Turkish edition of my book is here presented, with these minor additions, to our scholarly world.

One final word. I personally consider it a very pleasant task to offer, in a short time, to the criticism of specialist historians and sociologists who are occupied with the study of not only the problems of the founding of the Ottoman Empire, but also more generally with numerous problems of Islamic social history, a new volume to supplement this short book. It will contain the recent results that I have obtained by making use of almost all the Western and Eastern studies that have been made between 1934 and 1960 related to this subject. It will also cover the most important aspects of a number of historical problems concerning the present topic, on which I have either still not been able to publish {my findings} directly, despite forty years work in this field, or I had simply presented them rather briefly in the present book. {The work that Köprülü promised was never published.}

Fuad Köprülü

1

THE QUESTION OF THE FOUNDING OF THE OTTOMAN EMPIRE AND HOW IT SHOULD BE STUDIED

After the collapse of the state of the Seljuks of Anatolia under the pressure and oppression of the Mongols of Iran in the second half of the thirteenth century, a new political entity appeared in the fourteenth century on the Seljuk-Byzantine frontier in the extreme northwestern corner of Anatolia. Within a short time, less than a hundred years, it developed into a powerful state that ruled the Balkans and a large part of Seljuk Anatolia. The profound and lasting consequences that arose from this phenomenon can be considered one of the most fundamental issues of the history of the later Middle Ages. This subject, however, has not yet been properly addressed. It has not been rescued from the tales recorded by the medieval annalists and has remained an enigma until today.

In recent years, after the appearance of H. A. Gibbons' book entitled *The Foundation of the Ottoman Empire* (Oxford, 1916), the question of the founding of the Ottoman state has become the subject of research and disputes among Orientalists. Clément Huart, in the articles that he published concerning this book in *JA* and *Journal des Savants*, expressed certain reservations about its conclusions but generally accepted them and claimed that, thanks to this work, "we have escaped from the childish tales surrounding the beginning of Ottoman history."[1] The German Turkologist F. Giese, in an article that he wrote about this book, accepted some of Gibbons' conclusions but strongly criticized his basic theory about the founding of the Ottoman state and advanced some new ideas of his own.[2] Somewhat later, Rudolf Tschudi,[3] W. L. Langer and R. P. Blake,[4] and finally J. H. Kramers, who wrote the article on the Ottomans in *EI*[1],[5] studied this question to some degree. In addition to their work, a number of publications on certain points related to this problem have appeared in other places. Unlike Gibbons' book, however, most of them were not able to go beyond the narrow confines of the world of the Orientalists and remained unknown to historians in general. Nevertheless, despite all these works, which are satisfactory neither in quantity nor quality, and the optimistic conclusions of Huart, we must admit that the mystery surrounding the founding of the Ottoman state is still far from being solved.

It is for this reason, therefore, that this problem has been selected, which is as important as it is unknown, as the subject of this series of lectures. I will first summarize and criticize the most widespread opinions on this topic in order to show clearly our current elementary state of research. Then I will try to explain the kind of method one should follow, to the extent that the existing sources allow, in order to be able to shed light on this subject. And finally, I will attempt to present—in the most general fashion without going into detail—the results that can be reached according to this method and the questions that need to be answered but have not yet received attention. I do not claim to be able to solve quickly, especially in the limited framework of a few lectures, a puzzling problem like the founding of the Ottoman Empire, which up to now has not escaped from the traditions of the medieval annalists. Instead, it will be a great satisfaction to me if I can succeed in eliminating certain mistaken views on the founding of the Ottoman state and replace them, at least partially, with rational solutions.

A. Gibbons' Theory: Summary and Criticism

The most widely favored view today in Europe, not only among Turkologists, but also among historians in general, concerning the question of the founding of the Ottoman state is that of Gibbons.[6] After the Great War {i.e., World War I}, we find that he is always used "as the basic authority" on this subject, even, for example, in the general history series published in France. The author, who no doubt exerted great effort to produce his aforesaid work, succeeded in examining a number of secondary problems related to political and military history in a more serious manner than previous historians had done. He even made correct deductions about some fundamental questions. His idea, for instance, that the "Ottoman state was able to expand its territory in Anatolia only after the conquest of the Balkan peninsula" is quite right. Furthermore, he is also entirely correct in his opinion that "the Ottoman conquests in the Balkans were not raids made for the purpose of destruction and booty, but were part of a plan of settlement." Yet, despite these views, his basic thesis about the founding of the Ottoman state is too weak to be supported against the simplest historical criticism. Before proving this, let me first briefly describe the main features of his theory on this subject:

1. Ertughrul, the father of Osman, who gave his name to the Ottoman state, fled from Khwārazm in the face of the Mongol invasion. He was the chief of a small tribe which came to Anatolia in the reign of the Seljuk sultan ʿAlāʾ al-Dīn Kai-Qubād I and established itself in Söğüd, in the northwest of the sultan's territory.

2. Osman and his small tribe were pagan Turks who lived as herdsmen. After entering the Muslim environment, they accepted Islam like the Seljuk Turks who were their kinsmen. This new spirit immediately aroused in them feelings of *prosélytisme*. They forced the Christian Greeks who lived around them, and with whom they had friendly relations, to become Muslims. Before Osman converted to Islam, there were only four hundred warriors in his company. They spent a quiet, idle, peace-loving life in their own environment. However, within ten years, from 1290 to 1300, their number grew ten fold.

Their borders expanded until they came in contact with the Byzantines. In this way a new race appeared, the Ottoman race which took the name of its chief. From its beginning, this was not a purely Turkish race, but a new, mixed race which was formed by welding together local elements as they were found. Pagan Turks and Christian Greeks constituted this new race together by converting to Islam.

3. Within a short time the Ottoman population grew to a great number. This event cannot be explained by natural increase. It is also a mistake to think that their number was supplemented by newly-arrived nomads from the east, because Ottoman territory was in the westernmost part of Anatolia and any groups of people who might have gone there would have been settled and taken into service by the other Anatolian *beyliks* {principalities} located to the east of Ottoman territory. Therefore, this increase can only be explained by the mixing {of Osman's tribe} with the local element, which was overwhelmingly Greek.

4. The quick and firm establishment of the Ottoman state in the Balkan peninsula cannot be explained by the above causes alone. The conditions in Byzantium, the Balkan states, and the Western world at that time certainly had a great effect. In addition to these external factors, however, the powerful personalities of the first Ottoman sultans must be taken into account. Furthermore, the Christians who fell under Ottoman rule in the Balkan peninsula had not been "the neighbors of Muslims for centuries" like the Christians in Anatolia. Consequently, in the reign of Murad I, different means were found to Islamize the large number of Christians in this new region. Prisoners of war who accepted Islam were saved from slavery, but their number was very limited and did not assure Islamization. Therefore, the law of *devshirme* was introduced which formed the janissary corps from Christian children and brought about their compulsory Islamization. Rather than give up their children, the Greek and Slavic elements in the Balkans found it very advantageous to immediately convert to Islam.

> When we consider the fact that even in the fifteenth century the number of janissaries had not become particularly significant and they did not constitute the basic element of the army, then it is much easier to understand that the janissaries were only used as a means of conversion and were not an organization that was created to strengthen the army.

These then are the major ideas that are defended in Gibbons' book. It is clear that he tried to explain the establishment of the Ottoman state only by religion, and believed that the newly adopted religion created a new race, an Ottoman race. Before criticizing his evidence, it is necessary to state that an attempt to explain such a great and important historical event solely by a religious factor, that is, by "a one-sided explanation," even if it does contain some degree of truth, is contrary to the complexity of historical reality and is always inadequate. Furthermore, by always using the term "race" instead of "people," the author causes considerable confusion. Although the Ottoman Empire was a historical reality, there was never an Ottoman race. Indeed, no Ottoman people ever existed. Gibbons tried to present certain evidence from Ottoman sources to prove that the names "Turk" and "Ottoman" had referred to two races or peoples whose characters were completely different from each other—for this constituted one of his basic theses. But this is nothing but the result of a misunderstanding. According to the old annalists, the word "Ottoman," which was not an ethnic but simply a political term, always had the meaning of "a dominant or administrative class which was in the service of the state and earned its living from the state budget." I will return to this question in a more detailed fashion later. For now, let me examine the kind of evidence on which Gibbons bases his claim that Osman and his tribe were latter-day Muslims.

Gibbons has no real evidence to support this interpretation, one which Th. Nöldeke[7] and A. Rambaud[8] had previously accepted and which F. Babinger[9] and R. Grousset[10] have more recently espoused. Based on certain late ethnographic observations of very doubtful value, he says that "the Turkmen tribes of northern Syria were Muslims only in name," and that according to some annalists, "they were related to the tribe of Osman." But this proves nothing. Gibbons relies on two legends found in the old Ottoman chronicles as his strongest evidence in this matter. He knew of course that these were legends, but believed that such legends could be used, albeit with care and caution, for periods for which the historical documents were lost, because he believed that they contained the reflections of certain historical events altered in the collective imagination. These legends appear in different forms in the Ottoman chronicles. Indeed, in some of them Ertughrul is mentioned in place of Osman. These legends can be summarized as follows:

> 1. Osman spent one night at the home of a Muslim mystic, Shaikh Edebalı. Before going to sleep, the owner of the house brought out a book and put it on a shelf. When Osman asked what kind of book it was, he said it was the Koran. To a question about its contents, he answered, "it is the word of God which was brought to the world by the Prophet." Osman consequently took the book in his hand and stood reading it until morning. As morning approached, he dropped off to sleep. He had a dream in which an angel appeared and brought him the good news that because of the reverence that he had shown {to the Koran}, he and his descendants would become powerful and respected.
>
> 2. Osman wanted to marry the daughter of Shaikh Edebalı. The *shaikh* would not agree to this for two years. One night while sleeping in the shaikh's home, Osman had a dream: A crescent rose from the breast pocket {*koyun*} of Edebalı and entered Osman's breast. A tree then grew from Osman's navel. The shade from its branches covered the entire world. Edebalı interpreted the dream and said Osman's family would rule the world. Then he gave his daughter to Osman.

As Giese rightly stated when he criticized Gibbons, it would be extremely rash to attempt to reach any conclusions about "Osman's conversion" from these legends. At the very most, one could see in them "a desire to give a divine legitimacy to the Ottoman family for the establishment of hegemony over the other Turkish tribes in Asia Minor."

Although Giese's observation is undoubtedly correct, I would like to examine this question a little more closely and show the kind of mistaken deductions that can be reached in this respect if "internal criticism" of the old chronicles is neglected. This might be considered, perhaps, an unnecessary digression within the limited and general framework of these lectures, but it is needed in order to fully elucidate the nature of the legends which form the basis of Gibbons' manner of explaining the founding of the Ottoman state. At the same time, this will show what great caution must be exercised in using the information that the Ottoman chronicles give on this early period.

In the *Ṭabaqāt-i nāṣirī* by the thirteenth century historian Jūzjānī, we find a tale which is similar to the legend according to which a tree sprang from Osman's navel in a dream and spread its shadow over the whole earth. Sebük-Tegin, the father of Maḥmūd of Ghazna, the conqueror of India, had a dream an hour before the birth of his son. In this dream, a tree grew from a brazier in his house and cast its shadow over the entire world. An interpreter of dreams explained this to mean that "he would have a conqueror for a son."[11] We find another version of this legend of the tree which appears in a dream in the section containing the traditions of the Oghuz in the great work of Rashīd al-Dīn, namely, his *Jāmi*ᶜ *al-tawārīkh*, the first universal history, which he wrote at the beginning of the fourteenth century at the court of the Ilkhānids. Here a certain Toghrıl and his two brothers are mentioned among the legendary rulers of the Oghuz. Before they founded a state, their father had a dream in which three large trees sprang from his navel. The trees grew and grew. They cast a shadow in every direction and their tops reached to the sky. He described this dream to the tribal soothsayer and asked him to explain it. The soothsayer, who had already announced that a great ruler would appear from within the tribe, warned the man saying, "your children will become rulers, but you must not reveal this secret to anyone."[12]

One more example. The motif whereby a family will have a great future because of respect for the Koran is also found in a small *saljūqnāme* from the fourteenth century, a source that predates the Ottoman traditions. When Lokman, a forefather of the Seljuks, was going to get married, seven copies of the Koran, which according to the custom of the time were given as part of the trousseau, were placed on reading stands in the bridal chamber. Lokman would not enter that chamber out of respect for the Koran. Those who saw this suggested that the books be removed and taken to another place, but Lokman did not think that this was proper. So the bridal chamber was moved to another house and he entered it. That night he saw the Prophet in a dream. Because of the respect that Lokman had shown to the Koran, the Prophet prayed for him and his children to acquire prosperity and glory in this world and the hereafter.[13]

One frequently comes across such dream stories in both ancient and medieval chronicles, beginning with Herodotus. The prototype of Osman's dream is clearly seen in the above legends. The Oghuz tradition recorded by Rashīd al-Dīn had either existed as an oral tale among the Anatolian Turks and then passed from this popular form to the Ottoman chronicles, or, perhaps with greater likelihood because of the considerable importance given to Rashīd al-Dīn's work at the Ottoman court in the fifteenth century, this tradition was taken directly from it and ascribed to the Ottoman family.[14] The description that is given below of religious conditions in Anatolia and among the Turkmen tribes at the beginning of the fourteenth century will show even better how untenable is Gibbons' point of departure.

There are more such general legendary motifs in the early Ottoman chronicles. For instance, in the story of the conquest of Bilecik {in northwestern Anatolia}, we have the motif of men who hid among the cargo {destined for the city} and thus slipped into the fortress. Different versions of this motif are found in the Muslim stories about the conquest of Samarkand,[15] in the *Ṭabaqāt-i nāṣirī*,[16] in the Anatolian story of Dānishmend Ghāzī, one of the famous conquerors of Anatolia,[17] in the *Zafernāme* of Sharaf al-Dīn ʿAlī Yazdī, which contains material about Tīmūr,[18] and later in Evliyā Chelebī's *Seyāḥatnāme*.[19]

In an attempt to find additional evidence to support his arguments and make them more forceful, Gibbons states that there was absolutely no historical record of the tribe to which Osman belonged—and other tribes like it which fled before the Mongol invasion and came to Anatolia—being Muslim. In his view, the Seljuk Turks who were established in Anatolia after the battle of Malazgird were true Muslims, but the tribes which fled before the Mongol invasion and appeared on the borders of Anatolia at the beginning of the thirteenth century had never fallen under the powerful influence of Islam, even though they had lived for several generations on the frontier of Iran. The small tribe to which Osman belonged had only given up its old paganism and adopted Islam after moving to the Muslim Turkish environment of western Anatolia. These opinions of Gibbons, who had no information at all on the religious conditions in Anatolia in the thirteenth and fourteenth centuries, are, in numerous respects, as unfounded as his claims based on the aforesaid dream. Moreover, although Gibbons had no idea at all about the ethnic formation of the Turks and the manner in which they established themselves in Anatolia, he believed that the name "Seljuk" was an ethnic term—exactly like the term "Ottoman"—and was not a political term taken from the founder of the dynasty. But there is a more fundamental mistake here than this, which must be clearly described in order to demonstrate in particular how indefensible is Gibbons' explanation of the establishment of the Ottoman state.

First, it can by no means be considered as an historical axiom that the tribe to which Osman belonged was one of those which fled before the initial Mongol invasion and came to Anatolia in the thirteenth century and established itself there. The information given in this regard in the early Ottoman chronicles, the oldest of which has been shown to date from the last part of the fourteenth century, are totally unworthy of belief. And Gibbons, by the way, who was no Turkologist, had absolutely no knowledge of the oldest and most important of these chronicles. In the sources for the Seljuk period, there is no record whatsoever that such migrations to the western regions of Anatolia took place at that time. As explained below, in light of our present knowledge, it is much easier to conclude that the tribe to which Osman belonged was one of those which had come to Anatolia during the very first Seljuk invasion.[20] Gibbons' great error has been embedded for centuries in the old Ottoman chronicles and in the old European works based on them. It was usually accepted as a fact by all Eastern and Western authors who discussed Ottoman history after J. von Hammer{-Purgstall}. It would therefore be unfair to attribute the responsibility for it to Gibbons. He saw no need, however, to criticize this tale, which had been created by the mentality of the medieval annalists, and wanted to use it to prove his own theory.

But this mistake pales in significance compared with a second error, which I will now describe. This misguided idea was to imagine that the Ottoman state merely arose from a small "nomadic or semi-nomadic tribe composed of 400 tents," and to try to explain, based on this erroneous and simplistic view, a very great historical event, like the founding of the Ottoman state. This approach to explaining the rise of the Ottoman Empire, which has been repeated uncritically from the old Ottoman chroniclers all the way to Gibbons—and could not even be discarded after him by Eastern and Western historians because of the inertia of simple custom—is contrary to positive thought and the historical mentality. The medieval chroniclers, in conformity with their own theological mentality, explained this miraculous event by supernatural causes, like the dream legend for example. In the twentieth century, however, there is no reason to continue to be satisfied with the same kinds of explanations—no matter how much one wishes to impose, in a more positive manner, certain forced interpretations. In order to maintain his hypothesis, Gibbons remains strongly committed to the story that the Ottoman state arose from a people of 400 tents. Were there no Turks who had come to Anatolia before or with the Ottoman tribe and joined the Ottomans? Could such a small and primitive tribe create on its own an organization to compete with Byzantium, no matter how weak it was, and rule the Balkans? Gibbons has no difficulty finding answers to these elementary and logical questions, which immediately come to mind, and defending his own hypothesis at the same time. Instead of relying on a single historical document and taking into consideration the historical conditions in Anatolia at that time, he makes new erroneous deductions based on the mistaken premises that he had presented: "Before the end of Orkhan's reign, the nucleus of Asiatic adventurers which had gathered around Osman in the little village of Sögüt had grown to half a million. It could not have been by natural increase. It could not have been by the flocking in of nomads from the East. Orkhan was cut off from contact with the Asiatic hinterland. His rivals, that is, the other Anatolian beyliks, wanted to attract adventurers from abroad before he did. Orkhan formed his nation from the local elements as they were found. These were mostly Greeks {p. 63}." After stating that these local elements formed the Ottoman race by adopting Islam, the author adds that the elements required to create the state organization "were found among the Greeks who were more capable of doing this than the nomadic Turks." In this way, he answers our aforesaid questions. This view, which had been current among Western historians before Gibbons, continues to be repeated even today as an axiom.[21]

As will be described below, his entire series of conclusions consists of a *préjugé*, a fantasy which does not accord at all with historical reality. Among the great men of the Ottoman state who won fame in the fourteenth century, and even the fifteenth century, there were very few Christian converts, like the family of Köse Mikhal for instance. Not only was the bureaucracy, which had been established according to Seljuk and Ilkhānid practices, composed entirely of Turkish elements, but those at the head of the government and army were also almost invariably Turks. All the historical documents in our possession show this to be definitely the case.[22] The decline in the power and influence of this Turkish aristocracy which administered the state, and the coming to power of the devshirme children who displaced it, began primarily in the second half of the fifteenth century. It makes no sense to attribute this transition {"to the fact that"} "nomadic Turks had no ability to establish the organization for a state," for it resulted from completely different causes and was necessary for an absolute empire established over various elements. Even if the small tribe of Osman had been nomadic or semi-nomadic, the Ottomans certainly would have discovered during the initial founding of their state, that is, at the beginning of the fourteenth century, that urban life among the Anatolian Turks had sufficiently developed so that they could easily find the necessary elements for the administrative machinery of their newly-established state among the Turks who had gained experience in the administrative organizations of the Seljuks, Ilkhānids, certain Anatolian beyliks founded before the fourteenth century, and even of the Mamlūk Empire of Egypt and Syria. Completely contrary to Gibbons' claims, we can say that the border area in which the Ottoman state developed was attractive enough to lure, for many reasons, a certain number of emigrant caravans from different places in Anatolia, indeed, to attract not only nomads but also urban dwellers.

Saying this, I do not wish to deny catagorically that Muslim missionary activity was present among the local Christian element in the Ottoman sphere of power. I cannot agree, however, that this Islamization was as prevalent as Gibbons alleges, especially in the fourteenth century. And I consider myself competent to describe as mere fantasy his hypothesis that this Islamization created—completely separate from the Turks—a brand new race or people who "formed the nucleus of a great state." His claim that the Ottoman state created the devshirme system only to Islamize the Balkans is, as Giese again has rightly criticized, a personal opinion that does not accord in any way with historical reality.

Giese has shown rather clearly—although not in the most convincing and well-argued manner—the baselessness of the kind of explanation advanced by Gibbons for the founding of the Ottoman state. Furthermore, he has maintained in turn that the organization of the *akhīs* {members of a religious fraternity, see ch. 3}, whose social significance in Anatolia in the fourteenth century was described very well by Ibn Baṭṭūṭa, played the greatest role in the founding of the Ottoman state. In his view, "Osman's father-in-law Shaikh Edebalı, a great many of Osman's comrads in arms, and even Orhan's brother ʿAlāʾ al-Dīn Pasha were members of this organization. This powerful religious group was of enormous help to the first rulers in founding the Ottoman state. The *yaya*, which was their earliest military organization, imitated the uniform of the akhīs. When the janissaries were established in the reign of Murad I, these new soldiers preserved the headgear of the akhīs."[23] Even before Giese, Huart had rightly pointed out that one should not neglect the question of the role of the different {*ṣūfī*, i.e., mystical} brotherhoods and the akhī organization in the founding of the Ottoman state. In an article that I published in 1922, before Giese's article, on Islam in Anatolia, I described the religious conditions in the Seljuk period, from the time the Turks adopted Islam, and at the time of the founding of the Ottoman state. In the process, I indicated the important role played by the akhīs, more than the other brotherhoods, and the influence they and the Bektāshīs had on the organization of the janissaries.[24]

Although I cannot concur with some of Giese's other ideas, and have previously expressed my opinion concerning them,[25] it must be conceded that, by pointing out Gibbons' mistakes and emphasizing the role played by the akhīs, the German scholar has helped give a new direction to the problem. He says, "It is necessary to abandon the erroneous idea according to which Osman independently laid the bases of the Ottoman state with only a Turkmen tribe of 400 tents." This, in fact, is where the question stands, merely presented in this fashion. But trying to eliminate the false premises at the heart of any problem is to take a step toward solving that problem.

B. The Conditions Necessary to Study the Problem in a Logical Manner

Everything that has been said suffices to show how backward is the research on the founding of the Ottoman Empire. After dispensing with Gibbons' one-sided explanation based on myth—the prototype for which we found in sources older than the Ottoman chronicles—our information on this great historical event of the late Middle Ages essentially goes no further than it did at the time of Hammer. Frankly speaking, we have not even saved ourselves from the naive stories of the old Ottoman chroniclers. Without doubt, thanks to the results obtained from the research that has been done for a century on the medieval West and Byzantium, we know incomparably better than in Hammer's time the situation in the Balkans and Byzantium and the external factors that facilitated the rapid growth of Ottoman power in the Balkan peninsula. This is clearly of great help to us in understanding the origin of the empire. But it is also an equally obvious fact that, in order to solve this problem, it is necessary to recognize, above all, the internal factors.

Ethnically, to which branch of the Turks did those who founded the Ottoman Empire belong? When did they come to northwestern Anatolia and settle there? What was their social status? Were they nomadic, semi-nomadic, or settled? To what extent were the elements {of the population} which increased in number and social significance Turks? To what extent were they non-Turks? What was the ratio between the elements which came from abroad and the local elements, and what were their mutual relations? How large was the nomadic element compared to those of the villagers and city dwellers? In addition, what was the relationship between Christians and Muslims?

How much power did the various social classes have and how much did each participate in the founding of the empire? Was the Ottoman Empire a democratic organization or an aristocratic organization? To what kind of transformation was the concept of sovereignty subject in the fourteenth century? What was the level of material and intellectual civilization? There are thus a great many fundamental questions about ethnography, religious history, legal history, economic history, in short, material and intellectual history, for which we must first acquire adequate documentation.

Moreover, not only do we not understand these internal factors, but we also do not understand a great many external factors, namely, the historical conditions of the Near East in the fourteenth century, a knowledge of which is indispensable in order to comprehend the development of the empire. The roles that the state of the Golden Horde and the Turkish {Mamlūk} Empire in Egypt and Syria played in Anatolia during the period in question are also poorly known. The relationships of the different Anatolian beyliks to each other, to the Ottoman state, and to these foreign states are also insufficiently known. Under these circumstances, faced with all of these unknowns, is it impossible to try to solve the problem of the origins of the Ottoman state? Until now, not one of those who has taken up this problem, and Gibbons is no exception, has subjected the questions that I have posed to serious study. Indeed, not one of them has even thought of subjecting each of these questions to study.

Because of this, it is to be regretted that, with regard to the level of historiography, the work that has been devoted to the medieval Orient has not gone beyond the narrative form which is content with describing political and military events. The results of the studies on the early history of the Ottoman state in particular, even with regard to merely political and military events, are very poor, simplistic, and usually contradictory. Is it necessary, however, to attribute the cause of this, as Gibbons has done, to the fact that we possess inadequate sources? Does this lack of material make it impossible to do serious research on the questions that I have raised? Is the problem of the founding of the Ottoman Empire doomed to remain insolvable like a system of incomplete equations? I do not believe so. In order to prove my point, I will first try to define the nature and value of the material in our possession. Then I will show how it should be used with the application of the proper method.

1. The Sources

It is true that the Islamic sources for the history of Anatolia in the fourteenth century, the century in which the Ottoman Empire was founded, are few and inadequate. If we disregard certain works of minor importance written in the Ilkhānid period, certain passages of the Egyptian chroniclers and biographers, and the observations of Ibn Baṭṭūṭa on Anatolia, we can say that works which were produced as historical sources for this century, and which were completely devoted to Anatolia, do not in fact exist. And as for the few sources we do have, which even today exist for the most part in manuscript, Gibbons could only use those which had been translated into Western languages. These translations, moreover, generally consist of misread and misunderstood texts which are relied upon uncritically—Orientalism not having advanced to date as far as research on the ancient periods—and are therefore untrustworthy.

In any case, in addition to the above sources, we can use important works related to this period, like {Rashīd al-Dīn's} *Jāmiᶜ al-tawārīkh* (partially unpublished), {ᶜAbd Allāh b. ᶜAlī al-Kāshānī's} *Tarih-i Uljaytu*, and then {al-Qalqashandī's} *Ṣubḥ al-aᶜshā* and {Ibn Saᶜīd's} *al-Taᶜrīf* {see *Selçuklu tarihi, Alparslan ve Malazgirt bibliografyası* (Ankara, 1971), p. 14, nr. 91}; and finally works which were written in the fifteenth century but contain important information on the fourteenth century, like *Tarih-i ᶜAinī* {i.e., al-ᶜAinī's *ᶜIqd al-jumān*} and {Ibn Ḥajar al-ᶜAsqalānī's} *Durar al-kāmina*.

As for the sources written in Anatolia in the fourteenth century, although they are extremely limited, they have been used very little up to now. We can consider Maḥmūd b. Muḥammad al-Aqsarāyī's Persian history entitled *Musāmarat al-akhbār* to be the oldest and most important of them. This work, two manuscripts of which are found in Istanbul (Ayasofya Library, MS 3143, Yenicami Library, MS 827), is composed of four parts. The last of them, which mentions in particular the Ilkhānids and the last Seljuk rulers under their protection, and which frequently relies on the observations of the author, is extremely important. This part constitutes two thirds of the work. The *Muṣāmarat al-akhbār* was written on behalf of the Ilkhānid governor of Anatolia, Demirtash b. Emīr Choban in 723/1223. Among the early Ottoman historians, only Müneccim-başı saw and used this important chronicle. For a while it attracted the attention of Professor W. Barthold,[26] but it has still not been properly used.[27] Next comes the great work called *al-Walad al-shafīq*—of which a unique manuscript is found in the Fatih Library, nr. 4519—written by Qāḍī Aḥmad of Niğde in 733/1332. Up to now, it has not been used at all. In this work, which is a kind of encyclopedia of the different Islamic sciences, there is information on Seljuk history as well as very valuable material on the religious and social history of Anatolia in the fourteenth century. The author, who states that he wrote a great history of the Seljuks—unfortunately this work has not come to light—briefly describes their state here among the other Muslim dynasties. But with the exception of the information given on the last rulers, this material cannot be considered particularly important. With respect to social history, however, this text has great value. In addition to these works, we have the great chronicle entitled *Bazm u razm* which ʿAzīz b. Ardashīr Astarābādī wrote on behalf of Qāḍī Burhān al-Dīn, the Sultan of Sivas.[28] This text, which was published by the Türkiyat Enstitüsü in 1928, is the most important source in our possession on Anatolia in the last half of the fourteenth century.[29] If we add to these works a short *saljūqnāme* in the Bibliothèque Nationale (coll. Ch. Schefer, nr. 1.533 pers.; E. Blochet, p. 131), which has been studied by Th. Houtsma[30] —and which for some reason was not known to Gibbons—we will have exhausted the major sources written in Anatolia on fourteenth century Anatolia.

We can supplement these texts with a few late works written in the fifteenth century, namely, Shikārī's book of rather doubtful value on the history of the Qaramānids[31] and Enverī's *Düstūrnāme*, which apparently used an old source on the history of the Aydınids and which has recently been published by Mükrimin Halil Yınanç.[32] The latter work, which is the most important source on the Aydınids, is not without value for Ottoman history in the fourteenth and fifteenth centuries.

Furthermore, we do not lack other Islamic sources to which we can refer for {information about} Anatolia in the fourteenth century: secretarial handbooks, literary and mystical works of various kinds, *waqf* {pious endowment} documents, collections of the legends of saints, and the like.[33] An example of the last type of work, that by Aflākī, was translated and published by Huart under the title *Les saints des derviches tourneurs*. After publishing this work, Huart recognized its importance as an historical source for religious events and subsequently presented some of the information that he had gleaned from it in a short article that he published in *JA*.[34] I have previously demonstrated that the information given in this work on the Anatolian beyliks, when compared with every other kind of historical document, has the ring of authenticity.[35] I would not claim that all the works on the legends of the saints are of the same importance and trustworthiness as Aflākī's, but it could be said that these kinds of works, no matter what they are, if subjected to careful criticism, are basic sources for research on social history.

In any event, from this rapid review it is quite obvious that, although they are limited, there exist a number of important sources on the history of Anatolia in the fourteenth century. The epigraphic and numismatic research that has been done in the past 25 years, especially in Turkey, has also produced rather important results for this period.[36] Nevertheless, Western researchers who have worked on the question of the founding of the Ottoman state, and, unlike Gibbons, knew the Oriental languages, indeed, even the Orientalists, have not made proper use of the sources that I have mentioned. This being the case, the reason why no serious studies have been done on the social history of Anatolia in the fourteenth century is self-evident. It is clearly a mistake to attribute this merely to the lack of material or inadequate sources. In order not to cause any misunderstanding here, let me clarify one point in particular: until now, not one of those who has specifically tried to study and explain the problem of the founding of the Ottoman state has felt it necessary to do research on it in the context of the general history of Anatolia in the fourteenth century, and consequently they saw no need to do basic research on the sources mentioned above. All their efforts and attention were focused on only one point, that is, to try to solve the problem of the origins of this state by finding sources that were devoted exclusively to it and to the Ottoman dynasty and using those sources alone! An attempt to understand this great problem within such a narrow framework, namely, to find sufficient sources on fourteenth century Ottoman history and try to reach a conclusion based on them, will inevitably lead, as it has to date, to a dead end.

Gibbons, who was carried away by this mistaken approach and attempted to study and explain the problem within such a narrow context, says that there is no early Ottoman source on the origin of the Ottomans, that their oldest chroniclers were from the end of the fifteenth century, and that Byzantine and Western historians naturally could not provide reliable information on the first humble appearance of the Ottomans. Gibbons did not know any more about the earliest sources of Ottoman history written in the Ottoman Empire than had been described by Hammer, but he is essentially correct in these observations.

Although considerable research has been done on the early Ottoman chronicles since 1916, and many new texts have been published, the situation is not much different today. The great majority of the new sources presently in our possession were never seen by Gibbons or even Hammer. They include ʿĀshıq Pasha-Zāde's *Tarih* {*Tevārīh-i āl-i Osman*} published in two separate editions by Ali {Istanbul, 1332} and Giese {Leipzig, 1929}, the anonymous *Tevārīh-i āl-i Osman*, Uruj Bey's *Tarih* {*Tevārīh-i āl-i Osman*} edited by Babinger, Lutfī Pasha's *Tarih* {*Tevārīh-i āl-i Osman*} published in Istanbul, the *Behcet ül-tevārīh* by the historian Şükrullah and edited by Th. Seif {in *MOG*, 2 (1923–26)}, and Karamānī Mehmed Pasha's *Tarih* {see *İA*, s.v. "Mehmed Paşa,

Karamānī" (M. C. Şehabeddin Tekindağ), p. 591} and Enverī's *Düstūrnāme* both published by Mükrimin Halil Yınanç. In addition to these works, the section on Ottoman history that the poet Ahmedī added to the great romance called the *Iskendernāme* written in verse at the end of the fourteenth century, Bihishtī's *Tarih* {see *EI*[2], s.v. "Bihishtī" (Ménage)} and Rūhī's *Tarih* {see *İA*, s.v. "Rūhī" (M. K. Özergin), pp. 764–65}, Ibn Kemal's {or Kemal Pasha-Zāde's} *Tarih* {*Tarīh-i āl-i Osman*}, various anonymous manuscripts called *Tevārīh-i āl-i Osman*, Konevī's {i.e., Mehmed Emīn Ibn Ḥājji Halil's} history of the Ottomans and other such sources, which were not known to Hammer, are not unknown to the scholarly world—although they are still unpublished.[37] Even if we add to these texts certain anonymous handbooks of chronologies,[38] some *kānūnnāmes* {digests of sultanic laws} which have been published in Istanbul and Vienna,[39] and a few very rare official documents,[40] and if we take into account the epigraphic and numismatic research that has been done on the Ottoman period in the last 25 years, we will have a better appreciation of the scarcity and inadequacy of the sources for fourteenth century Ottoman history.

With the exception of a few works from around the beginning of the first half of the fifteenth century, all chronicles were generally produced around the end of the fifteenth century or even later. The chroniclers relied on popular oral traditions or on purposely fabricated tales for the information that they provided on the early stages of the founding of the state, so their work is a kind of extension of early popular epics. It should not be forgotten that they copied each other with few differences among them.[41] In order to make use of them, we must always keep in mind the need to subject them to very strict historical criticism. I have mentioned, in particular, that official documents from the fourteenth century are very rare, because Mükrimin Halil Yınanç has clearly shown that the documents on the early periods in Ferīdūn Bey's *Münşe'āt*, which have been used up to now as a primary source for these periods—although there have been doubts about their veracity—had been completely fabricated.[42] In any case, the description above shows that a historian who knew these new sources, which were unknown to Gibbons, very well and could make full use of them, but who stayed within the same narrow context as Gibbons, would be in no better position to explain and solve the problem of the founding of the Ottoman state, for these new sources do not give us much different or more trustworthy material than what was already known about this early stage.

We should not expect to find much more than what was known in 1916 about the earliest periods from the other Islamic sources or Byzantine and Western sources. Critical editions of the Byzantine chronicles of the fourteenth century can correct some of our information on Ottoman history in this period—or perhaps some new documents will be discovered in, for example, the Italian archives which can shed light on certain problems of Near Eastern history in this century—but, whatever the case, we cannot logically expect authentic documents directly concerning the early stage of the founding of the Ottoman state to appear in Egyptian, Byzantine, or Western sources.[43]

Under these circumstances, what should one do about the inadequate Ottoman sources for the fourteenth century? By doing meticulous research on various categories of documents and certain literary and scientific works written under the Ottomans in this century, it is possible to elucidate to a degree some points that the chronicles have not been able to explain, especially those concerning social history. In my view, however, this would not be sufficient to explain this great problem. We thus come now to the basic point of my thesis. As I have tried to explain above, the fact that the question of the origins of the Ottoman state has presently reached an impass has resulted from not only the scarcity of material and inadequacy of sources, but above all from the mistaken manner in which the question was posed. This has led to an erroneous and simplistic interpretation of the problem, completely inappropriate to the historical mentality. As long as the complicated question of the origins {of the Ottoman state} remains bound to this traditional error, which is based on the old Ottoman chronicles and, strangely enough, is still current among all Eastern and Western scholars who have studied Ottoman history, it will be impossible to explain.

2. The Method of Research

After briefly discussing the narrow and simplistic nature of this mistaken and unrealistic point of view, which I have tried to demolish for a long time in the many works that I have published on the literary, religious, and legal history of the Ottomans, I would now like to show how the question of the founding of the Ottoman state should be presented and the kind of mentality and method that should be used to do research on it.

It is an inexcusable error, with regard to history, to attribute the founding of the Ottoman state to a tribe of 400 tents, established on the Seljuk-Byzantine frontier in the northwestern corner of Anatolia in the thirteenth century, without giving any thought to explaining this event within the political and social conditions of Anatolia in the thirteenth and fourteenth centuries. The geographic area in which the Ottoman state was founded was not like an isolated island in the middle of the Pacific Ocean. The people who lived there did not constitute an ethnic element distinct from the Turks of Seljuk Anatolia. When first Seljuk and then Ilkhānid rule was strong in Anatolia, they and the other Anatolian Turks formed a political, economic, and cultural unit. There was, no doubt, a difference in the living conditions between this group {i.e., the Ottomans} who lived on the marches, that is, the frontiers, and the Turks who lived in the inner regions. But this difference was not just confined to this group, for other Turkish tribes lived there as well. Their social composition was no different from that of the other Anatolian Turks. Whether nomadic, seminomadic, or completely settled, they had, without exception, the same living conditions as the Turkish tribes in Anatolia.

Even if we leave aside all these considerations and imagine, for a moment, that conditions were completely the opposite, we would still not be able to dispense with the need to study this question within the general framework of the history of Anatolia in the thirteenth and fourteenth centuries. The early Ottoman historians who eulogized the Ottoman dynasty not only invented wholly fictitious genealogies for the Ottoman sultans, who in fact were not related to the family of any ruler, but also tried to explain, through a series of legends, the founding of the Ottoman state by means of supernatural causes in order to show that it was completely miraculous. It was quite natural for annalists who wished to write an epic about this dynasty to depict Ottoman history as a series of such {supernatural} isolated events. Although modern historiography does not accept miracles or supernatural causes, it has sought {in this case} to continue the same tradition in different form. This is difficult to understand. As I have said on numerous occasions, if Ottoman history is viewed and analyzed in the context of Turkish history in general, that is, as a continuation of the history of the Anatolian Seljuks and the different Anatolian beyliks, only then will it be possible to elucidate a great many problems which have remained obscure up to now. The very poor knowledge that we have even today of the history of the Anatolian Seljuks is no doubt an obstacle to understanding this simple fact. Nevertheless, as long as the question of the founding of the Ottoman state is not presented in such a rational manner, it will never escape the impasse in which it is presently found, and thus, a great many basic problems of Ottoman history will not be possible to resolve. In a previous work, I described and analyzed at great length the many erroneous conclusions that a great many Byzantinists, from Rambaud to N. Iorga and Ch. Diehl, had reached about Byzantine-Ottoman cultural relations because they remained bound to a mistaken approach, like that of Gibbons, to the question of the origins of the Ottoman state.[44]

Now, after this fundamental fact is accepted as the starting point and the question is posed in this fashion, the road to be followed in order to explain and solve it will automatically become clear, namely, to subject the sources in our possession to internal and external criticism according to today's historical methodology; to refuse to attribute anything positive to the legends and genealogies that were fabricated for specific purposes by the annalists and to stop using them; to disregard doubtful events of political and military history and minor feats of arms which had no lasting results and devote attention only to basic questions; to not just remain bound to chronicles but give more, or at least as much, importance to other kinds of documents that could be of use in solving historical problems; and to do research on the stratification of the various elements which constituted Anatolian Turkish society in the thirteenth and fourteenth centuries, their positions with respect to each other, their strengths and weaknesses, the causes of antipathy or solidarity among them, in other words, to do research on the changes in the inner life of this society rather than show the continuous transformations on its surface. In short, we must create an historical synthesis by trying to determine the morphology of this society and the evolution of its religious, legal, economic, and artistic institutions more than its political and military events. Only such a synthesis—obtained by using every kind of available material—can give us the explanation of the problem of the founding of the Ottoman state that is the closest to historical reality.

Let me answer a question here that might immediately come to mind. Is the material in our possession of sufficient quantity and quality to make such a comprehensive synthesis possible? Without doubt, no! Let us remember, however, that, compared to those who have tried to explain the founding of the Ottoman state up to now with the legendary data provided by late Ottoman chronicles, we possess very rich material with which to attempt this synthesis. If we were to try, for example, to write an *annale* like an ordinary historiographer, which recorded year by year the events of the Ottoman state based on the sources presently in our possession, we could say that this would be materially impossible because we have no means at all of checking the trustworthiness of the information, all highly suspect, that the Ottoman chronicles give on this matter. And there is nothing to be found in the Byzantine and Arab sources, official documents, or inscriptions in this regard. Under these circumstances, we must cast aside without hesitation such doubtful material. After such a process of elimination, to be done according to the full requirements of historical criticism, the number of events whose authenticity appears to be relatively well established will be very small.[45] But the historian, unlike the annalist, does not need to know every event and every possible bit of information to satisfy his curiosity. There are thousands of minor, insignificant, and recurring events recorded in the *annales* and other historical documents a lack of knowledge of which would be no obstacle whatsoever to understanding the historical development of a society. Here we have the essential difference between a narrative history and a synthetic history. By saying this I do not deny the great importance of *érudition* in historical work. I only wish to call attention to the fact that a historical synthesis is completely different from an accumulation of material which has not been criticized—material the value of which is undetermined and in which the significant has not been separated from the insignificant. The goal of the historian is to explain the reasons for the progress of any society at a given time and place, and to bring it to life in the manner closest to reality by means of various manifestations of social life. His role is no different from that of a paleontologist who reconstructs from a few bones in his possession the basic skeleton of an animal whose species has been extinct for thousands of years. My purpose in repeating this point, which is an axiom, an obvious assumption, among modern historians, is to show that great use can be made of even the limited material in our possession to elucidate the problem of the origins of the Ottoman state; because those who have been occupied with this question until now, for the reasons that I have given above, have not been able to take advantage of the most important parts of this material.

In the two lectures which constitute the critical and methodological introduction, I will try to analyze and explain at least the general outline of the problem of the founding of the Ottoman state by making use of every kind of source that I have mentioned. The bold attempt at a synthesis that I want to make in a field in which virtually no work has yet been done certainly will not claim to give the final and absolute answer to this great problem. Even syntheses based on the most solid analytical work do not pretend to claim finality. One should expect no more than this from the present initial attempt at a synthesis, for which analytical research is still needed in a great many respects. The primary objective that I have kept in mind in these lectures is the following: to present in concrete fashion the need to apply to historical studies on the Turkish and Islamic Middle Ages the new methods which have been followed in historical studies on the Western Middle Ages since the nineteenth century. With very rare exceptions, this additional and important part of the history of mankind has still not escaped from the traditions of the medieval annalists despite all the efforts of nineteenth-century European Orientalists.

2

A REVIEW OF THE POLITICAL AND SOCIAL HISTORY OF ANATOLIA IN THE THIRTEENTH CENTURY AND THE FIRST HALF OF THE FOURTEENTH CENTURY

In order to understand the founding of the Ottoman state, it is necessary to know not only the political history of Anatolia in the thirteenth century, but also, above all, its social history according to the methodological principles that I described and discussed at length in the first lecture. Only by knowing the conditions of social life in thirteenth century Anatolia will it be possible to discover the material and moral forces that created the Ottoman state in the fourteenth century and made possible its rapid growth, and to understand the basic elements that constituted the substructure of this political entity. A great many conditions that existed in Anatolia in the thirteenth century, with regard to ethnic formation, social organization, economic order and cultural development, also continued, naturally with certain changes, in the fourteenth century. In any event, with respect to political changes, the thirteenth century was the most remarkable and active period of the history of medieval Anatolia. As a result, it was a time of transition and reformation—the effects of which would appear in the following centuries—regarding social crystalization. This phase of history was closely bound to the first half of the fourteenth century which was the early foundation period of the Ottoman Empire. The thirteenth century was the greatest political and cultural period of the empire of the

Anatolian Seljuks. It was the century in which the {Greek} states of Nicaea and Trebizond were established in Anatolia on the ruins of the Byzantine Empire after the Fourth Crusade; in which the Mongols became the de facto rulers of Anatolia and Seljuk rule became a shadow; in which the Anatolian Turks became part of the great Ilkhānid Empire; in which the Empire of the Golden Horde, the friend and ally of the Mamlūk Empire of Egypt and Syria, which was the rival of the Ilkhānids, attempted to play a political role in Anatolia; and in which the Byzantine Empire was resurrected in Constantinople. One can only understand the political circumstances which prepared the way for, and made possible, the founding of the Ottoman state in the first half of the fourteenth century, by studying and explaining them as a continuation of those of the thirteenth century.

It would have been impossible for such great political events of the thirteenth century not to have had a very profound effect on all manifestations of social life. The formation of a number of large ṣūfī brotherhoods, which were influential in Turkey for centuries, and the economic antagonism between the nomads and settled people, which manifested itself in the guise of a religious revolt that was so powerful that it shook the Seljuk state at the height of its power, were both consequences of all this. We also see the consequences of these events in the first half of the fourteenth century—indeed, even in later centuries. For all these reasons, let me now try to sketch a general and, as far as possible, clear picture of the history of Anatolia in the thirteenth and first part of the fourteenth centuries—not only the manifestations of political life but even more so the social institutions.

A. Major Political Events

The first half of the thirteenth century marked the zenith of the empire of the Anatolian Seljuks. In the second half of the twelfth century, they had eliminated the Dānishmendids, their most powerful and dangerous rivals, and then completely destroyed the relatively unimportant local dynasties like the Mengüjekids, Saltuqids, and Artuqids, or left them as rulers of subject principalities. Even Lesser Armenia, which, because of its geographic position, had been able to maintain its independence by complying from time to time with various rival powers, became a small subject state which was required to pay taxes and give military assistance. For purely economic reasons, Ghiyāth al-Dīn Kai-Khusraw I captured Antalya in 1207 and his successor, ʿIzz al-Dīn Kai-Kāʾūs I, seized Sinop in 1214. The Seljuk Empire thus obtained an outlet on both the Mediterranean and Black seas. It could enter direct commercial relations with the countries bordering these seas and was thus open to trade with Europe.

As for the political history of Anatolia, the principal change at the beginning of the century was the founding of the Empire of Nicaea with its capital at Nicaea and the founding of a coastal state on the Black Sea by the Comneni—with the help of Queen Thamar of Georgia—centered at Trebizond, both as a result of the Fourth Crusade. With respect to the general history of Anatolia, the establishment of the Empire of Trebizond did not play a prominant role in the general current of events.[1] There is no doubt, however, that the founding of the Empire of Nicaea was much more significant.

The Byzantinists say that this new empire with its capital at Nicaea had as its first priority, by its very nature, the need to maintain its territory in Anatolia and consequently it formed a powerful obstacle to the advance of the Turks toward the West in the first half of the thirteenth century.[2] In addition, Iorga is of the opinion that the Seljuk sultanate was in a state of decline when the Empire of Nicaea was established.[3] In my view, both of these interpretations are mistaken.

Around the time of the early formation of the Empire of Nicaea, the Seljuk state was frequently preoccupied with struggles for the throne among the princes because there was no established method of succession. Ghiyāth al-Dīn Kai-Khusraw I strengthened his internal position, took

Antalya, and then, at the urging of Alexius III Angelus who had taken refuge with him, attacked the emperor of Nicaea, Theodore I Lascaris, in order to place Alexius on the throne. But Kai-Khusraw was killed in battle in 1210.[4]

There is a considerable difference between the Seljuk historian Ibn Bībī and the narratives of the Byzantine sources concerning this war. Ibn Bībī does not mention anywhere that Alexius sought refuge with the sultan. He writes that the sultan decided to go to war because of his longstanding hostility to this new state on his western frontier. Thus, after passing through the region of Alashehir {Philadelphia}, which was in Greek hands, the Seljuk army met the army of Lascaris. The emperor fell from his horse in the first clash, but the sultan prevented him from being killed. When the Byzantine army saw this, it began to flee in confusion. As a result, even the company of soldiers who were always at the side of the sultan deserted him in their greed for booty. It was at that moment, adds Ibn Bībī, that a Frankish soldier killed the sultan by taking advantage of the fact that the sultan thought he was one of his own men and paid no attention to him. This soldier then put on the sultan's finely adorned garments and, when he returned to his own army, the Greeks realized that the sultan had been killed, regained their courage, attacked the Seljuk forces again and defeated them. According to the same author, Lascaris was very grieved by the sultan's death and tortured the Frankish soldier until he died. When ʿIzz al-Dīn Kai-Kāʾūs I ascended the throne, Lascaris sent an embassy to him with a great many gifts together with Emīr Saif al-Dīn Chashnīgīr, who had been taken prisoner in the battle, in order to establish friendly relations. The Seljuk sultan reacted favorably to this and sent Emīr Saif al-Dīn back to him as ambassador. In the meantime, his father's body was transported to Konya. Afterwards, ʿIzz al-Dīn moved against his brother ʿAlāʾ al-Dīn, recovered Antalya and, in agreement with the Empire of Nicaea, set out against the Comneni at Trebizond. On the pretext that they had attacked his territory, he took Sinop from them. He also made a punitive campaign against Lesser Armenia. ʿAlāʾ al-Dīn Kai-Qubād I, who succeeded him, always maintained friendly relations with the neighboring {western} empire. In fact, when the Mongol invasion began, both the Empire of Trebizond and the Emperor of Nicaea, John {III Ducas} Vatatzes, immediately recognized the need to unite {with the Turks} against this common danger. We know that later there were friendly relations between ʿIzz al-Dīn Kai-Kāʾūs II and Theodore II Lascaris. All of this reveals very clearly that the state of the Anatolian Seljuks did not adopt a threatening position toward the Greek state of Nicaea.

I also do not believe that the view advanced by A. A. Vasiliev, according to which Ghiyāth al-Dīn Kai-Khusraw wanted to expand toward the west in his war with Theodore I Lascaris, is correct. From the time that it was established, the Greek state of Nicaea had as its goal to take back Constantinople from the Latins and reunite and revive the fragmented Byzantine Empire. It fixed its gaze above all on the west, on the Balkans. It was, therefore, only interested in the coastal areas of Anatolia and the islands in the Aegean, that is, the former Byzantine territory. The Greeks could not dream of invading Seljuk Anatolia. Even for the Western world which had previously considered Anatolia to be "a country under Turkish occupation," in the thirteenth century this region had become simply "Turkey." Although it was so insignificant that it did not change the border between the two states, the fact that Lascaris' victory over Kai-Khusraw so pleased the Greek world is the clearest proof that the state of Nicaea was in no position to consider embarking upon a conquest to the east {i.e., it was satisfied with this victory}.[5]

As for the Seljuk Empire, the first half of the thirteenth century, especially the reign of ʿAlāʾ al-Dīn Kai-Qubād I, was, completely contrary to Iorga's claim, its most brilliant and powerful period. The capture, primarily for economic reasons, of Anamur, ʿAlāʾiyya {Alanya}, and a number of other fortified places on the southern coast of Anatolia; the dispatch of a military expedition to Soğdak, which was an important port in the Crimea; the punishing of Lesser Armenia; the capture of large parts of eastern Anatolia and very important military and economic centers like Kahta, Chemishkezek, Erzinjan, Erzurum, and Akhlat; the successful struggles against the state in Āzarbāījān and Iran founded by Jalāl al-Dīn the Khwārazm-Shāh after he had fled from the Mongols; and the construction of a great many buildings and public works all occurred at this time. For ʿAlāʾ al-Dīn, who had created a united and unrivaled power in central and eastern Anatolia and was more interested in obtaining the rich regions to the east than lands to the west, the major objective was to capture Aleppo and northern Syria. This had also been the goal of his predecessors. Although he did not, in fact, succeed in doing this, he alarmed all of his eastern neighbors and won considerable influence. Despite the appearance of the Mongol danger, his son, Ghiyāth al-Dīn Kai-Khusraw II, captured Samosata, Diyārbakr, and Mayyāfāriqīn and thus forced a number of neighboring princes and the Ayyūbids of Aleppo to recognize his sovereignty. All of this shows that the friendly attitude of the Seljuk and Nicaean empires toward each other had nothing to do with the weakness of the Seljuks but derived from the fact that one of them directed an active policy toward the west and the other toward the east, and their primary interests did not conflict. Indeed, each of the two empires benefited from the existence of the other for political balance. Neither side had any new reason to upset this balance, which had been established on the Seljuk-Byzantine border even before the thirteenth century. I will explain more fully a little further below, while describing the ethnological consequences of the Mongol invasion, how and why this balance broke down against Byzantium in the fourteenth century.

The most fundamental event in the history of Anatolia in the thirteenth century, not only politically but also socially, was the Mongol invasion. Thanks to the prudent policy of ʿAlāʾ al-Dīn Kai-Qubād I, this danger, which appeared on the frontiers of Anatolia around the end of his reign and greatly alarmed the Greeks as well as the Turks, was at first avoided. Indeed, thanks to his policy it even receded. This made it possible for Kai-Khusraw II to make new conquests in the east. His domestic administration, however, broke down. Some of the tribes of the Khwārazmian Turks who, after the death of Jalāl al-Dīn the Khwārazm-Shāh, had been established in Anatolia with their powerful chiefs by ʿAlāʾ al-Dīn Kai-Qubād, crossed the Seljuk border {i.e., left Seljuk territory} causing great damage and Kai-Khusraw had to struggle against them. All this, combined with the weariness caused by his ill-conceived and misdirected conquests, shook the state in spite of its outward brilliance. As I will mention below, the Bābāʾī revolt broke out at this time and greatly alarmed Kai-Khusraw, who crushed it with considerable difficulty.[6] It was at that moment that the Mongol danger appeared once and for all. In 1242, the Mongols captured and destroyed Erzurum. The Seljuk ruler met the Mongol invasion with a large force composed not only of his own men, but also reinforcements from allied and subject states. At the battle of Köse Dağ (1243), the Mongols inflicted a defeat on this heterogeneous army. They captured and destroyed Sivas and Kayseri and then turned back to capture Erzinjan, and withdrew again. It can be said that this war had a decisive effect on the fate of the Seljuk Empire. Afterwards Anatolia fell, in effect, under Mongol rule; although the peace which was made—on condition that a heavy annual tax be paid to the Mongols—left a theoretical semi-independence to the Seljuk sultan.

Political life in Anatolia was then subject to the will of the Mongol rulers: sometimes one prince from the Seljuk dynasty, sometimes another, or several of them together, were made sultans by the decree of the Mongol rulers {*khāns*}. Certain statesmen who had won the confidence of the Mongols and essentially took the Seljuk government into their own hands acquired greater power than the Seljuk rulers. The commanders of the Mongol occupation army in Anatolia oversaw the Seljuk government. In reality, they were the absolute masters of the whole country. Maintaining the ruler and Seljuk commanders {*emīrs*} on the one hand, and satisfying the needs and wishes of the Mongol army and high officials on the other, not to mention sending annual taxes and gifts to the leader of the Mongols, continuously increased the economic difficulties. Heavy taxation oppressed the people and thus caused widespread economic and spiritual distress. The complex administrative machinery of one system upon another, and their becoming enmeshed with each other, naturally functioned very poorly and always to the detriment of the people. There were rivalries between the Seljuk sultans and their emīrs, both of whom constantly intrigued with the Mongols against each other. Sometimes the Mongol commanders fought among themselves. There were revolts against their leaders. Punitive actions and wars followed the revolts.

These then were the kinds of events that filled the history of Anatolia in the second half of the thirteenth century and at the beginning of the fourteenth century. Before matters became so complicated under the energetic government of the great Seljuk statesman Muʿīn al-Dīn Pervāne, who had the support of the Mongols, the powerful ruler of the Egypto-Syrian Empire {of the Mamlūks}, Baybars, intervened in Anatolia—sincerely believing certain appeals—in order "to save Muslim Anatolia from the pagan Mongol usurpation" and marched as far as Kayseri. He inflicted a terrible defeat on the Mongol army at the battle of Elbistan, but Anatolia did not rise against the Mongols as he had imagined. In fact, he could not find any significant support and this dangerous situation forced him to turn back (1277).

The Ilkhānid ruler Abaqa came to Anatolia with a large army and killed thousands of people on the pretext that they had collaborated with the Egyptians. Indeed, in the end, even Muʿīn al-Dīn Pervāne was not able to escape {the same fate}. Afterwards the situation throughout Anatolia became grave and confused. Despite Baybars' lack of success, the Egypto-Syrian Empire of the Mamlūks, because of its geographic location and hostile policy toward the Ilkhānids, followed Anatolian affairs with great interest. One could assume that the Mamlūks more or less played a role in all the uprisings against the Ilkhānids in Anatolia. In both the rebellions of Sülemish, the commander of the Mongol forces in Anatolia in the thirteenth century, and that of Demirtash in the fourteenth century, the rebels always expected help from the Mamlūks.

There is also a strong likelihood that the Empire of the Golden Horde was no stranger to Anatolian affairs and probably played a role in these uprisings. This state was the natural ally of the Mamlūk Empire and we have begun to learn from recent studies that, in the second half of the thirteenth century, it put strong and effective pressure on the Balkans and on Byzantine policies. When the Mongol commanders in Anatolia marched from Ereğli {Heraclea} on the Black Sea toward the southwest and Byzantine territory in 1298, a force of Aq-Tav Tatars was sent, probably by Nogay {ruler of the Golden Horde}, to help Byzantium. They went to Anatolia via Gallipoli and, after they were defeated, returned to Rumelia. In any case, at that time the state of affairs was confused everywhere. A civil war broke out in the Golden Horde between Nogay and Toqtay {or Tokhtu}. In their second clash, the old Nogay, who had for long wreaked havoc in the Balkans, lost not only the battle but also his life (1299). The Byzantine Empire, which had remained free from Nogay's power, considered it prudent at that time to be on good terms with the Ilkhānids, probably to alleviate the pressure that was building on its Anatolian frontier. The revolt of Sülemish had previously saved Byzantium from this danger for a while, and later the protection of the Ilkhānid ruler Ghāzān did the same. Upon the death of Nogay, a Turkish people composed of 10,000 households which had crossed from Anatolia to Dobruja in 1263 under the leadership of Sarı Saltuk—that is, at a time when Byzantium had to accede to the policies of the Mamlūk and Golden Horde empires—returned to Anatolia again under the leadership of Eje Halil in order to join Sultan ʿIzz al-Dīn, and went back to the province of Karasi {Mysia, the province of Balıkesir}.[7] Future research should shed more light on the political roles of Egypt and the Golden Horde on the development of events in Anatolia.

In short, at the end of the thirteenth century, the Ilkhānid military administration in Anatolia increased its pressure daily, but despite severe punitive actions, it was unable to establish firm order. Ilkhānid rule was absolute in eastern and central Anatolia, mainly in the large cities on the commercial and military routes. However, in the mountainous regions which were easy to defend when necessary, and on the marches which were far from the major roads and where communications were difficult, this rule was rarely felt.

While the Seljuk state in Anatolia continued to decline under the pressure of all the internal and external conditions that I have described, it is worthy of note that, in certain favorable areas, some completely new Turkish powers began to crystalize. The earliest and strongest of them was that of the Qaramānids, which came into existence in western Cilicia, with Ermenek as its capital, after that region was captured in the reign of Kai-Qubād I. This power resulted from the unification of the Turkish tribes that had long lived in the mountainous regions of Cilicia with the Turkish element that had been transferred there by Kai-Qubād. In 1261, on the pretext of supporting ʿIzz al-Dīn Kai-Kāʾūs who had fled to Constantinople as a result of the intrigues of Muʿīn al-Dīn Pervāne, the Qaramānids marched on Konya but were defeated by Mongol and Seljuk forces. During the revolt of the Khaṭīrids, who were aided by the Egyptians, the Qaramānids defeated several Seljuk armies that were sent against them to relieve Konya. They then took advantage of the general confusion to seize Konya in 1277 and place an adventurer on the throne who claimed to be a son of Kai-Kāʾūs, but in the end they were again defeated by Mongol and Seljuk forces. Despite these blows, the Qaramānids, whom the Egyptians never ceased to support, continued to increase their power and influence. Initially having taken Konya while claiming to be the heirs of the Seljuk state, the Qaramānids captured that city on two more occasions at the beginning of the fourteenth century, but were driven out the first time in 1315 by Emīr Choban the *Emīr ül-ümerā* {commander-in-chief} of the Ilkhānids, and the second time in 1320 by Demirtash the son of Emīr Choban and governor of Anatolia. After Demirtash fled to Egypt and Ilkhānid rule in Anatolia weakened, the Qaramānid beylik developed into a powerful state with Konya as the capital.

Another power that took form on the western frontier

of Anatolia in the second half of the thirteenth century was the Germiyānid beylik. This beylik was established by the chiefs of a Turkish tribe that probably belonged to the Afshar branch of the Oghuz. Because of various factors arising from the Mongol invasion, this tribe had left the regions of Fārs and Kirmān and, perhaps in the company of the Khwārazm-Shāh, headed west. After his death, it remained for a while near Malatya. It then moved to the Kütahya area where it established itself. The rapid formation of the Germiyānid beylik recalls that of the Qaramānids. In 1283, upon the execution of Kai-Khusraw III by the Mongols and the placing of Ghiyāth al-Dīn Masʿūd II on the Seljuk throne, they rebelled on the pretext of supporting the slain ruler. They attacked the lands under Mongol-Seljuk rule directly to the east of them (1286). Masʿūd II came to crush them with an army composed of Mongol and Seljuk forces. Although he was at first victorious, he was attacked by surprise on his return and was routed. He came back the next year and defeated the Germiyānids, but when he withdrew they began to attack him again. The two sides tried to reach an understanding for a while, but it came to nothing and the struggle continued until 1290.[8] Afterwards, an agreement was reached between the Seljuks, or more correctly the Ilkhānids to whom they were subject, and the Germiyānids. Indeed, in 1299, it was agreed that Ankara would become a possession of the Germiyānids. It appears that when the Germiyānid *beys* {title of a prince, ruler, chief} were freed in this manner from difficulties on their eastern border, they began to attack Byzantine territory with all their forces and continuously tried to expand their own borders at the expense of Byzantium. When the famous Emīr Choban, the Ilkhānid Emīr ül-ümerā, came to invade Anatolia with a powerful army in 1314, the princes of the Germiyānid family and some of the powerful Germiyānid emīrs who were under their rule went to him with valuable gifts and declared their allegiance to the Ilkhānids.

All the historical sources for the fourteenth century record that the Germiyānid beylik was a very strong and important political entity, that a number of other Anatolian beyliks recognized its sovereignty and feared it, and that even Byzantium paid it an annual tribute. As I have previously tried to explain, the Aydınids in Ionia, the Inānjids in Laodicea, the Karasids in Mysia and, I would guess, even the Ṣārūkhānids in Lydia, all established beyliks that were subject to the Germiyānid state, at least in the early period of their foundation. Their founders were emīrs of the Germiyānid state. The Ṣāḥib Atāids at Karahisar were forced to rely on the Germiyānids in order to maintain their existence and acknowledged Germiyānid sovereignty. The Ḥamīdids in Pisidia had to rely on the Germiyānids to protect them against Qaramānid attacks. Altogether, it can be said that the Germiyānid state, whose hegemony over the beyliks in western Anatolia in the first half of the fourteenth century is also apparent from Byzantine sources, expanded its eastern border at one time as far as Ankara and for a while even possessed certain parts of Paphlagonia. Byzantine sources considered the ruler of Paphlagonia, Umur Bey, to be the possessor of the northern coast of Anatolia from the mouth of the Sakarya River to the lands of the Empire of Trebizond, and tell of his continuous struggle with the Greeks. I would therefore guess that this must be the Umur Bey whose name is mentioned in an inscription belonging to the Germiyānids and who was related by marriage to the Germiyānid family. {He was originally one of the commanders of the Germiyānids. It was only after his death that the Jāndārids were able to found a beylik in Paphlagonia (in Fr. ed.).} If this hypothesis were to be confirmed, and for now there is no evidence to the contrary, the size of the area under the influence of the Germiyānid state around the beginning of the fourteenth century will be better understood.

If we add the beyliks of the Hamīdids and Eshrefids in Pisidia and the Jāndārids in Paphlagonia to the political entities that began to crystalize in Anatolia around the end of the thirteenth century, we would complete the enumeration of the most important political formations of this period. Ḥamīd Bey was a Seljuk emīr who made Eğridir the capital of his beylik. Although its borders were considerably ex-

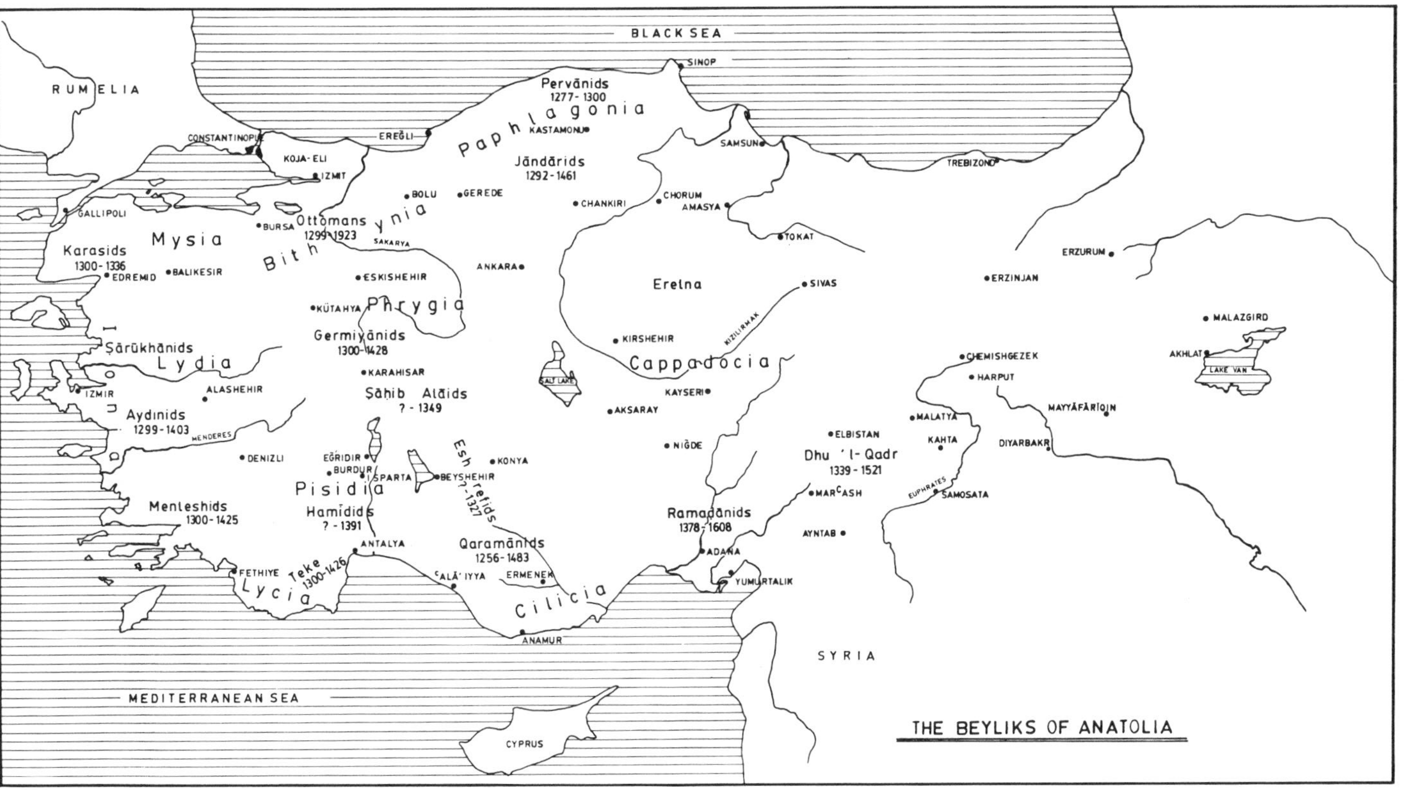

THE BEYLIKS OF ANATOLIA
BLACK SEA
MEDITERRANEAN SEA
RUMELIA
SYRIA
CYPRUS
Paphlagonia
Bithynia
Mysia
Phrygia
Lydia
Ionia
Pisidia
Lycia
Cilicia
Cappadocia
Pervānids
1277-1300
Jāndārids
1292-1461
Ottomans
1299-1923
Karasids
1300-1336
Ṣārūkhānids
Aydinids
1299-1403
Germiyānids
1300-1428
Ṣāḥib Alāids
? - 1349
Eshrefids
? - 1327
Hamidids
? - 1391
Menleshids
1300-1425
Teke
1300-1426
Qaramānids
1256-1483
Erelna
Ramaḍānids
1378-1608
Dhu 'l-Qadr
1339-1521
SINOP
EREĞLI
KASTAMONU
CONSTANTINOPLE
KOJA-ELI
IZMIT
SAMSUN
TREBIZOND
BOLU
GEREDE
CHANKIRI
CHORUM
AMASYA
TOKAT
GALLIPOLI
BURSA
SAKARYA
ANKARA
EDREMID
BALIKESIR
ESKISHEHIR
ERZURUM
ERZINJAN
SIVAS
KÜTAHYA
MALAZGIRD
KIRSHEHIR
KIZILIRMAK
AKHLAT
LAKE VAN
CHEMISHGEZEK
HARPUT
KARAHISAR
SALT LAKE
KAYSERI
IZMIR
ALASHEHIR
MAYYĀFĀRIQIN
AKSARAY
MALATYA
ELBISTAN
MENDERES
KAHTA
DIYARBAKR
NIĞDE
DENIZLI
EĞRIDIR
KONYA
BURDUR
ISPARTA
BEYSHEHIR
MARCASH
EUPHRATES
SAMOSATA
AYNTAB
ANTALYA
ADANA
FETHIYE
ʿALĀʾIYYA
ERMENEK
YUMURTALIK
ANAMUR

panded by his grandson Dündar Bey, it was later abolished by Demirtash, the governor of Anatolia. Only after his flight to Egypt was it able to revive, and the territory that had previously belonged to the Eshrefids also passed into its possession. The Teke beylik in Lycia also belonged to a branch of this family. Demirtash had put an end to the existence of the Eshrefid beylik in and around Beyshehir, but it was reestablished by another Seljuk emīr. In any case, these were strong principalities like those of the Qaramānids and Germiyānids, but their political role was not as important. As for the Jāndārid beylik which possessed Paphlagonia and a large part of the northern coast of Anatolia, it was a state that followed a skillful policy of striking coins in its own name only after the death of the Ilkhānid ruler Abū Saᶜīd Bahādur Khān. It became one of the politically powerful entities of the first half of the fourteenth century.[9]

All of this shows how much the territory of the Ilkhānids, and of the Seljuk rulers who were dependent upon them, had shrunk by the end of the thirteenth century. After Öljeitü Khudā-Banda ascended the Ilkhānid throne at the beginning of the fourteenth century, the governorate of Anatolia was created as a means of putting an end to the confused state of affairs there. This is evidence that the Ilkhānid Empire was anxious about this region. The coming of Emīr ül-ümerā Choban to Anatolia to straighten out its affairs and, after Abū Saᶜīd Bahādur Khān ascended the throne, the dispatch of Choban's son Demirtash to the Anatolian governorate with a large force ensured order for a time. Demirtash, who dealt harshly with oppressors but generally won the affection of the people with a benevolent and just administration, wanted to play the role of a *mahdī* {restorer of religion and justice who will rule before the end of the world} in Anatolia with the help of the Mamlūk state with which he had established secret relations. In 1322, he rebelled, but was defeated and forgiven by his father. Although he returned to his former position, he was forced to take refuge in Egypt upon the execution of his father, and Anatolian affairs became confused once more (1327). Around that time, Konya definitely fell into the hands of the Qaramānids. An inscription in Ankara dated 1330 shows, however, that the sphere of Ilkhānid influence still reached as far as that city. But the Ilkhānids probably only had real power at that time in central and eastern Anatolia. The western and southern regions had been absorbed by the Turkmen beyliks, the most important of which I have mentioned above.

My brief description of the founding of these small states suffices to show that they were not—as has been believed—new political entities that immediately came into existence on the ruins of the Seljuk Empire after its demise at the beginning of the fourteenth century. By taking advantage of the laxity and tolerance of Ilkhānid government, these states appeared gradually as local powers in the second half of the thirteenth century. They were the manifestation of an historical development the duration and significance of which depended on their geographic location and the abilities of their leading personalities. Some of them, for example the Germiyānid, Menteshid, Aydınid, Ṣārūkhānid, Karasid and Ottoman beyliks, were founded, and then expanded, by conquering territory from Byzantium, which by that time was slowly disintegrating because of a great many internal and external difficulties. It was not possible for the other beyliks which were not located on the marches to develop to the same extent. The Germiyānid beylik, which was a strong political entity, was itself eventually surrounded by more recent states that were established on the frontiers by its own commanders. It thus became an interior state {with no outlet on the frontier} and could not continue to develop because of pressure from powerful neighbors like the Qaramānids.

My purpose here is not to go into an explanation of the factors in the development or decline of the various beyliks in Anatolia, but only to show that the beyliks on the marches, of which the Ottoman beylik was one, had more potential for expansion. Because a great many important events which took place on the eastern borders of Anatolia after the decline and collapse of the Ilkhānid Empire were far away and had no repercussions on the historical development of western Anatolia for a rather long time, I see no need to mention them here in order to explain the occurrence of the founding of the Ottoman Empire. Furthermore, the internal and external conditions of the Byzantine state in the second half of the thirteenth century and the first half of the fourteenth century are clearly known, at least in a general manner. Consequently, instead of going into more detail on the political history of that period, let me try to describe, from the ethnic, legal, economic, religious and cultural points of view, the essential internal process of the life of that time—only the external manifestations of which we see—and its constant elements and basic motivating factors.

B. Ethnic Factors

It is not very easy to provide a general sketch of the ethnic landscape of Seljuk Anatolia, or determine the status of its population, either before or after the appearance of the Mongols. No research, even tentative research, has been done in this regard. We cannot, to be sure, obtain adequate material on this subject from the limited historical documents in our possession. However, because it is necessary to get an idea about this matter, albeit approximate, for the history of this period, let me present here, on the one hand, the results of a synthesis of the historical and geographic documents and, on the other, the results of a synthesis of our knowledge of the toponymy of Anatolia.

A great many Turkish tribes that came to Anatolia before and after the appearance of the Mongols established villages in their own names in the places where they settled. They also brought to the areas to which they came the names of a number of villages, mountains and rivers from the places where they had previously lived. An analysis of these place names, which still exist in Anatolia, in a systematic manner, that is, with the help and strictures of both linguistics and history, can suffice to elucidate this important problem which cannot be resolved by historical documents alone.

The settlement of Anatolia by massive groups of Turks who came from the East began in a regular fashion under the patronage of the Great Seljuk Empire after the victory at Malazgird, especially during the reign of Malik-Shāh. On his order, Süleyman, who is considered to be the founder of state of the Seljuks of Anatolia {Rum}, established Turkish tribes on the steppes of central Anatolia. Indeed, there were even a number of raids toward the northwest and southwest coastal regions. After the initial successes of the Seljuk state, a great many large groups of the Oghuz who lived in Central Asia, primarily in the areas beyond the Sayhun (Jaxartes) and between the Aral and Caspian seas, came to Iran. Some stayed there while others advanced further west, concurrent with the expansion of the Seljuk Empire in that direction, in the hope of finding empty lands which could assure them better living conditions. This massive and continuous Turkish migration, which started from Central Asia, was the major factor that made the conquest of Anatolia take on the nature of a systematic settlement instead of being a temporary raid or military operation. The Great Seljuk Empire, which rapidly developed into a well-ordered state in Iran by immediately adopting the administrative organization surviving from the Sāmānids and Ghaznavids, could not allow this torrent of immigrants flowing from the south of the Caspian Sea to break against the Iranian plateau. Running in all directions from there, this torrent could have ruined the social and economic system of what was then the rich area of Iran. In other words, it could have upset the empire. The conquests of Toghrıl, Alp-Arslan, and above all Süleyman, gave a definite direction to this flood of immigrants.

We find that the migratory movement toward Anatolia continued throughout the eleventh century and in the early years of the twelfth century, although it was not as intense at that time. During the settlement of Anatolia, the Seljuk Empire divided the large and powerful tribes into various sections and sent them to areas that were far apart. In this way, it hoped to eliminate the possibility of a revolt on the part of any strong, numerous, unified ethnic group under the direction of hereditary chiefs and, by breaking tribal solidarity, open the way to the creation of a national entity. It thus wished to protect the interests of the Seljuk family because the kinds of difficulties that could be caused by large, undivided ethnic units led by their chiefs had already been experienced at the very beginning of the invasion of Anatolia. The fact that in Anatolia today one comes across numerous villages, at some distance from each other, that bear any one of the names of the major branches of the Oghuz Turks, like Qınıq, Avshar, Bayındır, Salur, Baya'ut, Chepni, etc., is a consequence of the Seljuk method of piecemeal settlement. Other factors may have affected this, but the most fundamental factor was this policy of the Seljuk state.

Among the masses who came to Anatolia and settled after the Seljuk conquests, there were people belonging to various Turkish groups, like the Qarluqs, Qalaches, Qıpchaqs, and Agacheris, but the Oghuz Turkmen constituted the vast majority. Furthermore, they encountered in Anatolia a number of blocks of Christian or pagan Oghuz and Pechenegs whom the Byzantine Empire had brought from Rumelia and had established on the borders. Still, it is certain that in the thirteenth century Anatolia suffered a considerable loss of population, for this was a period characterized by continuous fighting—the Crusades, struggles between the Turks and Byzantium, and internal warfare between various Turkish rulers and commanders. The Turkish element was not the only one to be affected by this. Groups of other elements which had hastened to Anatolia from different areas of the Muslim world for such reasons as the lust for adventure, profit, and fighting for Islam, plus the earlier people of Anatolia—whom the Orthodox church had tried to Hellenize[10]—and the Greeks, who were in especially large numbers in the coastal areas, in short, all the people of Anatolia were affected by this. According to a story told by Abū ʾl-Fidā, which probably predates the Mongol invasion, a Turkmen people of 200,000 tents was living northwest of Antalya in and around the Denizli Mountains, that is, in the environs of the Menderes River.[11] It could probably be said that by the end of the twelfth century, Anatolia, with the exception of the western regions and coastal areas, had been fairly extensively Turkized by a large mass of Turks—more than were in northern Syria, Iraq, al-Jazīra, and in the area of Iran and Āzarbāījān.

The appearance of the Mongols caused a large new migration from the East to the West. This increased to a considerable degree, the concentration of Muslim Turks in the areas that I have mentioned above, especially in Anatolia which was the westernmost region of the eastern Islamic world and proved to be the safest place from this new invasion. In addition to a great many nomadic tribes which were in the path of the Mongols, numerous more or less prosperous villagers who had been able to emigrate because they possessed transportable wealth, rich merchants, intellectuals, artisans, and wandering dervishes went especially to Anatolia and settled there. They were attracted to this region by both its geographic position and the fact that the sultans of the Anatolian Seljuks still maintained the prestige of the Great Seljuk dynasty, and Anatolia, under the rule of a powerful state, was at that time a flourishing, wealthy Muslim country with favorable living conditions.[12] We know that after the collapse of the Empire of the Khwārazm-Shāhs, and above all after the death of the Khwārazm-Shāh Jalāl al-Dīn, a number of powerful Qanghlı and Qıpchaq tribes came to Anatolia under the leadership of their chiefs and entered the service of ʿAlāʾ al-Dīn Kai-Qubād I, and that, as a result of the bad government of Ghiyāth al-Dīn Kai-Khusraw II, they crossed the Seljuk frontier {i.e., left the Seljuk state}, overrunning and devastating the areas before them. It appears from a toponymic analysis, however, that some of them probably remained and settled in Anatolia.

After the first caravans of emigrants who fled before the Mongol invasion, we find that there occurred several additional migrations after the Mongols made the Anatolian Seljuks recognize their sovereignty. Sometimes the sending of military forces to Asia Minor for various reasons led to the establishment of a number of Mongol and Turkish tribes in different areas, because the forces that were sent as garrisons were, in fact, sent with all their baggage, women and children to occupy certain areas which had been granted to them as *iqṭā*ʿs {grants of state lands or revenues by a Muslim ruler in exchange for service, usually military}. In addition, we know that even before Hülegü, the founder of the Ilkhānid state, a number of Mongol and Turkish tribes came from the East to Āzarbāījān, Iran and eastern Anatolia, and that Hülegü came with a force based on a people of 200,000 tents, approximately one million people (1253). It is also known that at various times a number of elements from the empires of Chaghatay and Jochi entered the Ilkhānid sphere and that during the reign of the Ilkhānid ruler Arghun (1284–91) the Ak-Koyunlu {White Sheep} and Kara-Koyunlu {Black Sheep} Turkmen moved from Central Asia to Anatolia and Ājarbāījān en masse. It is clear from both an historical and toponymic analysis that a significant portion of all these groups were established in Anatolia. The Ilkhānids began to transfer tribes, mostly Turco-Mongol, to Anatolia for military purposes mainly after Baybars' futile invasion.

It is mentioned in the historical sources that groups belonging to seven Mongol and Turkish tribes were established in different areas. The names and areas of settlement of only three are given: the Bisvuts around Aksaray, Kayseri and Konya; the Uighurs around Sivas; and the Chavdars in the regions of Ankara, Eskishehir and Kütahya. It is reported that the Bisvuts and Uighurs raised 10,000 armed men and the Chavdars 30,000.[13] Furthermore, it also appears from the historical sources that many other Turco-Mongol tribes, like the Samagars, Chaykazans, Barımbays, and Alagöz were active in central Anatolia even in the fourteenth century,[14] and for a while the Barımbays established a beylik around Diyārbakr.[15] The Turguts and Varsaks, whose names frequently appear in the fourteenth and fifteenth centuries, and the Kara Tatars, who were later driven {back to the} east by Tīmūr, were among the powerful Turco-Mongol groups which arrived in the Ilkhānid period.

A toponymic analysis reveals that there were a number of other Turco-Mongol groups which came to Anatolia and settled there in this period. Among them were some which came south via the Caucasus and by sea from southern Russia. Because they arrived in the Ilkhānid period, these tribes were usually referred to as "Mongol" in the historical sources, but a significant part of them were not Mongol but Turkish, as appears to be the case from anthropological observations and ethnic names. After the collapse of Ilkhānid rule, the Mongol elements, which were quickly and easily Turkized among the Turkish majority, entered the service of different beyliks according to their geographic location. Western sources confirm the existence of Mongols in the army of the Qaramānids in particular.[16]

All of this explains how, after the appearance of the Mongols and, above all, after Ilkhānid rule had been established in Anatolia, the large Turco-Mongol groups which came to that region increased to a great extent the Turkish majority there.[17] When the information provided by historical and geographic documents from around the beginning of the fourteenth century is compared to that given by Marco Polo on the ethnic situation in thirteenth century Anatolia, it is immediately obvious how strong the Turkish Muslim majority became within the short interval of a half-century.[18] The new nomadic tribes that the Ilkhānid government moved to eastern and central Anatolia forced the Turkish tribes which had lived in those regions for some time to withdraw to mountainous areas far from the military roads and to the western marches of Anatolia. In this way, there began a new advance of the Turkmen toward the coastal areas that were still subject to the Byzantine Empire.

This advance was not like the Seljuk invasion during the initial conquest of Anatolia, which rapidly extended to the shores of the Aegean and Sea of Marmara and was a military occupation of extensive regions inhabited by foreign {i.e., non-Turkish} elements who were left defenseless by the annihilation of the Byzantine army in Anatolia. In fact, shortly after this initial invasion, the Comneni, with the help of the Crusaders coming from the West, succeeded in retaking Bithynia, Ionia, Lydia and the major coastal cities in both the north and south by expelling the Seljuk forces. The local conditions, however, were now completely different. The Turks had first established themselves in the villages and cities in central Anatolia and then, as the inevitable result of the {increase in} population density, had advanced to the west in order to acquire new areas in which to live. They descended from the high plateaus and mountains to the coastal areas. Indeed, there were already some Turkish groups in those areas. They had remained there since the time of the original invasion by accepting Byzantine rule or, for one reason or another, had emigrated there in the thirteenth century and had entered Byzantine service. There were also Christian or pagan Turks whom the Byzantine Empire, as the Empire of Nicaea was later to do, had brought from the Balkans and established on the frontiers. If Byzantium had at least been strong enough to protect its borders in Anatolia as Ilkhānid rule weakened there, the dense population created in central Anatolia by the Mongol invasion would not have been able to find an outlet to the west. This could have caused continuous clashes between city dwellers and nomads or among various groups of nomads and, as we have seen to some extent in previous centuries, forced certain nomadic elements to settle in Byzantine territory and enter Byzantine service in order to find rich pastures. However, because of different internal and external factors, Byzantium was too weak at that time to protect its Anatolian borders. Consequently, despite the skill of its diplomacy, which for centuries had excelled in the practice of destroying enemy forces by getting them to fight each other to its advantage, Byzantium could do nothing at all against this final invasion that advanced in slow deliberate steps. All the internal and external conditions of the period made this invasion inevitable.

C. A Brief Outline of the Social and Economic History

I have tried to explain perhaps the most important morphological factor of the Turkish pressure that drove Byzantium from its last territories in western Anatolia in the last years of the thirteenth century and especially in the fourteenth century. But this factor, no matter how important, cannot be separated from the need to study the other social factors that are useful in explaining a very complicated historical process like the founding of the Ottoman state. Thus, let me try to sketch for this purpose, in broad outline, the social life of the period whose political transformation has been already described.

With regard to their way of life and living conditions, the Anatolian Turks, who, under the name Seljuk in reference to the name of the reigning dynasty in the thirteenth century, formed a powerful political entity in the Near East, can be studied in three separate groups.

1. Nomads

Nomads, that is, the element that lived one place during the summer and another place during the winter (which was, more correctly, the semi-nomadic element), lived primarily by raising herds of animals, although they devoted themselves to some agriculture to meet their own needs. They supplemented this with earnings obtained fom the art of carpet weaving, which they brought from Central Asia, and from transporting goods. They were the ones who, at that time, raised the celebrated Anatolian horses and wove the very famous Anatolian carpets. The summer and winter quarters of these tribes, which lived under the leadership of hereditary chiefs, were well-defined. During times of migration, however, they could not refrain from damaging or destroying the villages en route. Occasionally, for various reasons, there was also strife among many tribes.

Each year they were assessed a tax, which they paid to the state in kind, not in cash, according to the size of the herds that they raised. However, such a tax was probably not levied on the tribes which were established on the frontiers for military purposes and which were given summer and winter pastures there. When deemed necessary by the state, they joined the army under the leadership of chiefs called *il-başıs*. These warlike tribes, the women and children of which were also armed, exhibited great courage on the frontiers. In the second half of the thirteenth century, the Chepni tribe, which had been established in the region southwest of the Empire of Trebizond, successfully repelled an attack by Trebizond on Sinop. The nomads on the frontiers did not hesitate to raid and plunder enemy territory whenever they found an opportunity.

Bertrandon de la Broquière, who went to Bursa in the first decade of the fifteenth century via the Hama-Antioch-Adana-Konya road, provides some very important information on the life of the Turkmen in southern Anatolia. He speaks of their moral qualities with great admiration.[19] This information can also shed light on the way in which the Turkmen tribes lived in the thirteenth and fourteenth centuries.

Unfortunately, I cannot go into any explanation here of the internal organization and legal system of these tribes which constituted the purest and most vigorous element of Turkish Anatolia. I can state, however, that these undisciplined masses recognized no social structure outside the tribal system, which was alien to the concept of a state, and despised the villagers and city dwellers. Whenever the central government weakened, they would immediately rebel and provoke anarchy. They did not hesitate to attack, pillage, or destroy open villages, cities which could not easily be defended, and commercial caravans. Numerous factors affected this behavior, but it was primarily economic destitution, sometimes caused by the greed and abuse of tax collectors, sometimes by the ambition and self-interest of tribal chiefs, and sometimes by the loss of their herds to drought or other conditions.

The historical information that we possess on the early period of the Qaramānids clarifies these points for us very well. The Seljuk rulers tried to find a solution to these rebellions by conferring official titles on the chiefs of certain tribes which they had subdued by force, and by placing some members of their families in the palace service as de facto hostages, but they were usually unsuccessful. Even in periods when the central government was at its strongest, fortress-like caravansaries possessing formidable defensive works were built on the busy commercial roads in order to prevent sudden raids by nomads despite the fact that commercial caravans were always protected by armed forces and garrisons were stationed on the roads to maintain public order.

Although these Turkish tribes were generally Muslim, they were free from all fanaticism and adhered more to a simple form of their old native traditions, which had the external luster of Islam, than to the obligations of a religion which for them was very obscure and impracticable. In fact, they were under the moral influence of extremist ʿAlawī or heterodox Turkmen *bābās* {"father," honorific title especially used in dervish circles}, who were nothing but an outwardly Islamized continuation of the old Turkish shamans. These nomadic tribes, whose religious mentality was much different from that of the settled people—as explained below—because of the economic and social differences between them, carried out a well-known general uprising, called the Bābāʾī insurrection in the historical sources, which was the largest movement in which they participated in the thirteenth century. Bābā Rasūl Allāh, who declared that he was the Messenger of God, and had a great many disciples among the Anatolian Turkmen, gave the order for the uprising in the area around Kefersud and Marʿash during the reign of Kai-Khusraw II. Because the Turkmen believed that he would one day declare a holy war, they had prepared themselves for it for some time. With dreams of booty and paradise in their eyes, these massive nomadic groups, including their women, children, and herds, attacked the villages and cities. They inflicted terrible defeats on several Seljuk armies that had set out against them, and they took control of the areas around Malatya, Tokat, and Amasya. The local Turkmen in these areas joined them. The Seljuk sultan did not feel safe in Konya and took refuge in the Qubādiyya fortress. One of his armies succeeded in capturing and hanging Bābā Rasūl Allāh, but it too was routed by the Turkmen in open battle. Finally, another army, which was hastily summoned from the eastern frontier and was composed of assorted elements, was able to crush this terrible uprising in a bloody manner (637/1239–40).

I have previously described at length the deep roots of this movement in Anatolia, its appearance in an area which had long been inhabited by the Paulicians, and its immediate causes and major consequences.[20] I showed for the first time that both the Bektāshī movement and a number of heterodox movements among nomads, which continued in Anatolia until the seventeenth century and were closely related to the founding of the Ṣafavid Empire in Iran, were connected with it.[21] Because I will describe a little later how such religious phenomena and religious groups were very closely related to the founding of the Ottoman Empire, I do not wish to dwell on the religious aspect of this insurrection here. The reason that this important event in the history of thirteenth-century Anatolia is mentioned, is to show more clearly the powerful potential of nomadic tribes as a military force, and their economic and social incompatibility with settled people.

It is not at all unlikely that Bābā Rasūl Allāh's movement was encouraged by the Khwārazmian tribes, which had been driven from Anatolia by the mistaken and hostile policy of Kai-Khusraw II and then went to the regions of Ayntab and Aleppo, by certain Ayyūbid princes, and by the Mongols who had assumed a threatening position on the frontiers of Anatolia. The fact that in 639/1241–42 a large force of Turkmen, namely, seventy thousand infantry and many cavalry under the command of Duduoghlu, joined the Khwārazmians sheds further light on the question of Bābāʾī links with the Khwārazmians. In the event, Bābā Rasūl Allāh assessed the internal and external conditions of the empire very well and gave the order for the insurrection while all its forces were busy in the east. This shows that he was a skillful politician. Furthermore, the concurrent increase in taxation because of continuous warfare, the decline in economic conditions, the breakdown of internal government, and the discontent of all social classes also explain why this insurrection took place at precisely that time.

These nomadic Turkmen who are described in the historical sources as wearing "black clothes, tall, red felt hats, and rawhide sandals"; the Turkmen who captured Konya under the command of the Qaramānids in the period of Mongol rule; and even the Turkmen who rebelled against the Seljuk Emperor Sanjar in Khurāsān in the twelfth century probably all represented the same social type. Because of the social antipathy between the settled people and nomads, one comes across vehement accusations, indeed, slander, against the nomadic Turkmen in works written by scholars who belonged to the bourgeoisie. Because I will discuss later the Anatolian marches, that is, the border areas, I will say no more here about the nomadic march tribes and pass on to a description of the villagers.

2. Villagers

The village class constituted a significant majority of the population of Anatolia. At the time of the initial Seljuk conquest, Anatolia was not heavily populated. The warfare which lasted for centuries between Byzantium and Iran, and then between Byzantium and the Muslims, had reduced the old population. The initial Seljuk conquest, the warfare of the twelfth century that followed it, and a life full of invasions were not immediately conducive to increasing the population. One could surmise, however, that village life slowly began to develop in the last years of the twelfth century. The non-Muslim population that the Seljuk conquest encountered in Anatolia had many ethnic origins and was partly urban and partly rural. To be sure, years of warfare and anarchy had brought hardship to both groups and had forced the defenseless village people into the cities, which were protected by fortresses, or into areas near the cities. After the period of warfare and anarchy passed, the Turkish rulers of course protected the non-Muslim farmers, because it was in the interest of the state to do so. Be that as it may, however, the rural population declined to a considerable degree. Therefore, in order both to solve this problem and prevent in advance the damage that massive groups of nomads could do, the Turkish states of Anatolia tried to transform them {i.e., the nomads} into villagers from the very beginning.[22]

I would like to dwell here a moment on an old and mistaken idea that has continuously caused a misunderstanding in Turkish historical studies. The large migrations that began with the founding of the Great Seljuk sultanate in Khurāsān did not bring only nomadic elements to Anatolia, for among the Turks who came to Anatolia there were all kinds of people who had adopted village life, indeed, city life, long ago in Central Asia.[23] Consequently, they maintained the same way of life in those places in which they had newly arrived. Villagers immediately established villages and began to farm. City people settled in the cities. It appears from the historical sources, and to a certain extent from a toponymic analysis, that the Turks came to Anatolia with some forces composed of elements of villagers and city dwellers from western Turkistan who were in the company of certain princes from the family of the *khāqāns* {supreme rulers} of Turkistan who were related by marriage to the Seljuks. Furthermore, in addition to Turks, many other Muslim elements, even certain Christian elements, came to Anatolia and established villages. However, because they were among a Turkish majority and under Turkish rule, they were gradually Turkized. Village life was most developed along trade routes, around large cities and towns, and in mining regions, but the villages along the major roads could not always be protected from destruction. Villages were in an especially difficult position if they were located on the routes to the summer and winter pastures of the nomads.

The Turkish village class that came from western Turkistan brought much of their farming culture with them to Anatolia, as they had to Iran. It is significant that numerous village and town names found there were brought to Anatolia and given to many newly established villages. Moreover, from the twelfth century to the present, numerous Turkish tribes which were basically nomadic were slowly and gradually sedentarized until they adopted village life. The Seljuk state, and especially the Ottoman state, exerted great efforts in this regard.

It cannot yet be said for sure whether or not village life in Anatolia declined or flourished in the Mongol period. The coming of a great many nomadic elements as a result of the Mongol invasion was probably not, however, in the interests of the village class and, at least for a while, prevented their development. In general, the villages exhibited ethnic or religious unity. Many villages were settled by people who belonged to a certain branch of a certain tribe and maintained their ethnic identity. Although nothing definite can now be said concerning the economic role of the villages in Anatolia, their social organization, and the kind of taxes they paid the state before the Mongol invasion, a few things can be deduced from the different documents in our possession. The village people were by no means a homogeneous class. In addition to a very limited number of farmers who worked lands that they owned themselves, there were those who were not landowners and worked as laborers in return for a certain wage or as sharecroppers using their own capital and labor on the land of another. They formed the great majority of the village population. Furthermore, there was also a village aristocracy—whose number in any village was very small—which held in their own hands a large part of the village lands and worked part of it with hired laborers and part of it with sharecroppers. They were the real rulers of the villages. They were a class that prevented contact between the people and the state. Although there were also village headmen or stewards {*kāhya*} who, in a way, were the representatives of the state, and especially the state finance office, and looked after matters concerning the common interests of the village, they were in fact the partners of the village aristocracy. Sometimes one or number of villages constituted the large estate of one person.

The Seljuk government was careful to revive, as much as possible, villages that were damaged or dissolved as a result of warfare and anarchy, and lightened or forgave their taxes for a certain time and even distributed seed for sowing and animals to work the land. We do not adequately know the kind and amount of taxes that were collected from the villages in the Seljuk period. It could be said, however, that, in its capacity as an Islamic state, the Seljuk sultanate collected the special tax {*kharāj*} from its non-Muslim subjects {*reāyā*}, a tithe {*uşr*} on all crops, and a number of village taxes which we know later existed in the Ottoman period—like the tax on the purchase and sale of land, and taxes on various agricultural crops and products—and levied tolls at highways or at guard posts at passes, bridges, or city gates on goods brought to market. These taxes also continued in the Mongol period, with perhaps some minor differences in the method of collection and the amount obtained. If any village or group of villagers was assigned a job that should be done by the state, such as operating a mine, maintaining a road, or repairing a bridge, it was exempt from taxes. As for pious endowments, which were highly respected in the Seljuk period, they were subject to certain attacks for a while in the early Mongol period, but they regained their former importance after Islamic influence became strong at the court in Tabriz. In short, the land regime was generally the same in all medieval Muslim states.[24] But instead of dwelling any longer on these points, which are well-known, let me go on to a description of urban life.

3. Urban Life

Culturally, the most important element was the city dwellers. One might easily assume that the initial Seljuk conquest and the events which followed were very disruptive of urban life in Anatolia for a rather long time. After the conquest, however, in the first half of the thirteenth century, the Anatolian Seljuk state consolidated its political and military position, gained access to the sea to the north and south, and created a well-ordered administrative system. Consequently, foreign as well as domestic trade flourished. The rulers took strong measures to protect commerce and this naturally was a major factor in the development of city life. Because it is not possible to learn about urban life and organization without knowing the extent of the development of commercial and industrial activity, let me try to describe this subject in the most general terms.

The Seljuk rulers clearly pursued an energetic commercial policy in the thirteenth century. They punished Lesser Armenia, which was located in an important transit area, for violating the security of trade caravans and forced it to pay an indemnity for all damages. Because of the importance of the ports of Antalya and ʿAlāʾiyya, they took control of the adjacent coastal areas. During the reign of Kai-Qubād I, an expedition was sent to Soğdak {in the Crimea} in order to establish secure trade for both Anatolian and Egyptian merchants—the latter having found the Alexandria-Antalya-Sinop route to be very safe—with the countries of present-day southern Russian and to make Sinop a commercial center. Because of the geographic location of the Anatolian Seljuk Empire, many international trade routes passed through it. This state controlled important centers like Diyārbakr and Erzurum, which were on the major Oriental trade routes, maintained security on all the roads, and instituted a kind of state insurance, the details of which are poorly known, against all types of losses. In short, it tried to obtain control of the transit trade. The establishment of the Empire of Nicaea unquestionably strengthened the economic relations of the Seljuk state with the Greeks, even though that empire at one time sought to limit or prohibit the export of certain luxury goods.

The Italian republics, which at that time occupied the most important position in Mediterranean and Black Sea commerce, entered into trade relations with the Seljuk Empire which had acquired new ports in those regions. Although it is known that Kai-Khusraw I, the conqueror of Sinop and Antalya, and his successors Kai-Kāʾūs I and Kai-Qubād I granted a number of concessions to the Venetians, the only record of this is found in a *ferman* {government edict} which has come down to us from the latter sultan dated 1220. It is also known that the Venetians sent an ambassador to Kai-Qubād I in 1228. According to the ferman, the Seljuk sultan gave the Venetian merchants permission to import precious stones, pearls, silver and gold (in coin or other form), and wheat without being subject to any tolls, and other goods on which a tax of only two per cent was levied. This agreement contained a number of stipulations which provided for the security of persons and property for the merchants of both sides. The sultan agreed not to interfere in commercial disputes between the Venetians and other Latins and the judges of the Seljuk state could only have jurisdiction in certain cases like theft or murder. In any case, this ferman shows that the Seljuk Empire gave freedom of trade to Christian as well as Muslim merchants within its own territory.[25]

There were Provençals who conducted the transit trade between Cyprus and the Konya sultanate. They imported mostly alum, wool, leather, raw silk, and silk textiles to the island.[26] But because the Seljuk sultans needed Latin mercenary soldiers and certain war engines—like those called *maghribi* catapults in the Oriental sources—for their armies, conditions favored the activities of Italian merchants in Anatolia.[27] In 1255, while returning from Karakoram, Rubruck encountered in Konya a Venetian and a Genoese who had both come from Syria. They had obtained a monopoly from the Seljuk state on the export of alum from Anatolia and were fixing the prices as they wished.[28]

It can be said that the movement of the Mongols into Anatolia, and Ilkhānid rule, had beneficial consequences with regard to the development of commerce despite the social disorder that they sometimes caused, not to mention the damage and slaughter resulting from military operations. To be sure, the foreign and domestic trade of the Seljuk Empire, which had established its influence over the Muslim principalities on its eastern frontier, showed signs of continuous strong expansion in the first half of the thirteenth century and the great prosperity of the cities on the major trade routes, like Konya, Kayseri, Sivas, and Erzurum, is striking. Although it may at first seem surprising, it can be claimed that this prosperity also continued under Ilkhānid rule. The Christian sources that mention Anatolia in this period, such as Marco Polo, Rubruck, and Haython, the Muslim sources for the thirteenth and fourteenth centuries, and finally the magnificent architectural works which survive from that time all testify to this. By being included within the borders of the great Ilkhānid Empire, Anatolia acquired a favorable position with regard to the movement of trade between Europe and Iran, for certain frontier barriers were eliminated. Because of its geographic location, Sivas became a commercial center at the intersection of a number of trade routes. Rich Muslim merchants who came from Konya, Syria, and al-Jazīra and Genoese merchants settled there. From Sivas, caravans were sent to the Black Sea ports, to Trebizond and especially to Samsun and Sinop. Sivas was located on the roads going to Tabriz, the urban centers of eastern Anatolia, the ports of the Mediterranean and Black seas and other areas of Anatolia, and was frequently the capital of the Mongol governors. After the destruction of the Latin principalities in Syria by the Mamlūks, the Christians made the port of Yumurtalık on the Mediterranean a first-class *entrepôt* for trade with the Mongols. The great commercial highway that connected Yumurtalık with the Sivas road and Tabriz is perfectly described by Pegolotti.

Trebizond and Tabriz were, of course, the most important centers of trade between Europe and Inner Asia and the Far East, but Anatolia probably profited as well from the economic policies of the Ilkhānid Empire. Tax revenue gradually increased. According to the historian Badr al-Dīn al-ʿAinī, the tax from Anatolia during the early Mongol oppression was 60,000 dinars, 10,000 sheep, 1,000 cattle and 1,000 horses; while according to the historian al-Aqsarāyī, when Bayju was in command of Anatolia this tax rose to 200,000 dinars. And this amount was maintained up to 1256. The revenues of Anatolia, which were 600,000 dinars at the beginning of the sultanate of Ghāzān, appear to have increased, according to the account of Ḥamd Allāh Mustawfī Qazvīnī, to 5,645,000 dinars, that is, 16,935,000 gold francs, in 1336—excluding the present-day western provinces of Anatolia and including parts of present-day Syria and Iraq. It is impossible to attribute this great difference in income from Anatolia, within the short time of less than a century, simply to an increase in taxes or similar reasons.[29] Around the beginning of the fourteenth century, the Armenian Haython points out that Turkey was a very wealthy country having rather rich silver and alum deposits, abundant wine, wheat and fruit, vast herds of animals and beautiful horses.[30] Later, Muslim sources from the first half of the fourteenth century mention the abundance and cheapness of everything in Turkey. In general, the economic level of the country had probably risen. Indeed, although Anatolia had experienced some economically harsh and depressing times, such as the period from Baybars' invasion to the sultanate of Ghāzān in particular, these sources show that afterwards the situation had improved. Because of its importance, this complicated problem needs to be subjected to strict historical criticism, that is, extensive study and debate. Let me leave it here and return to my description of urban life and organization.

In view of the course of political and social history, it would not be a mistake to trace the expansion of urban life in Anatolia back to the second half of the twelfth century and to suppose that it especially flourished in the thirteenth century. A great many of the old cities captured from Byzantium had, naturally, been populated from the start of the conquest, but the orderly arrangement of commercial relations, the concentration of industry in certain cities, in short, the transition from village economy to city economy probably occurred gradually. How were the first captured cities populated? How and why were new cities founded? Were these new cities established on the sites of certain abandoned cities? I will not discuss these questions which are as important as they are complicated. My purpose is only to say a few words about the development of urban life and organization in Anatolia from the thirteenth century to the founding of the Ottoman state, or more correctly, to point out the need to begin to do research on these subjects. For the sake of future historical research, it is essential to begin to try to explain these aspects of social history, which to date have not been studied at all, despite the very few or very fragmentary documents that exist. But before going into this subject, let me define precisely what I mean by the word "city." The meaning that I give to this word is very close to the term *ville* as used by Henri Pirenne while describing medieval cities.[31] In fact, it is almost the same, if we take into account the differences in character between the medieval Christian West and the medieval Muslim East. The city that I wish to discuss did not possess, like the ancient *cité*, an organization of tribal origin, the constitutional and municipal systems of which were indistinguishable from each other; nor did it resemble the *bourg* of the later Middle Ages. It is true, of course, that some Islamic centers, the founding of which we know about, like Kūfa and Fusṭāṭ for instance, more or less resembled a cité. One wonders if, in the early period of the Anatolian Seljuks, certain cities on the major military roads—like Konya, Erzurum, Sivas, and Kayseri—were founded in a manner roughly similar to that of the cité, from separate quarters composed of people belonging to the different Oghuz clans which were established next to the ancient towns which had been destroyed out of military necessity? For the time being, I find it prudent not to say anything about this matter. In the thirteenth and fourteenth centuries, probably none of the important cities of Anatolia resembled a cité in any respect. Like the Islamic cities of Baghdad and Aleppo, they were large commercial and industrial centers where people of different ethnic backgrounds, religions, social classes, and professions lived together. Beginning in the thirteenth century, we find that not only Turks, but also peoples of other ethnic origins and religions were present in large old cities like Konya, Sivas and Kayseri. Although Turks and Muslims formed the great majority, Greeks, Armenians and a few Jews were also found. Among the smaller cities and towns, however, there were some which were inhabited only by the Turkish element. Elsewhere, the proportion of other elements naturally differed with each city. Based on the historical documents in our possession, it is not possible to make even a rough guess about the size of all these elements and the changes they underwent.

Among the Turco-Muslim people who came from regions to the east after the appearance of the Mongols and during their rule were some who had maintained urban life for a long time and they settled in the cities of Anatolia. The Muslims of Semitic or Iranian origin found themselves among a Turkish majority and were quickly Turkized. People of different religions lived in separate quarters. Nevertheless, city life brought Muslim and non-Muslim elements very close together culturally and diminished the differences between them. When Mawlānā {Jalāl al-Dīn al-Rūmī} died, not only Muslims but also Christians and Jews attended his funeral ceremony.[32] A great many local customs and cult practices, the roots of which were in the pre-Christian period, survived among the local people whether Muslim or Christian.[33] The Greek and Armenian peoples of Anatolia who lived with the Turks learned Turkish. Furthermore, those among the Turks who knew the languages of these two peoples, especially Greek, were by no means rare.[34] The marriage of Turks to Greek and Armenian women had a considerable influence in this respect. In short, the people in the Seljuk cities exhibited virtually no difference among themselves with regard to material culture and there was no antagonism or outbreak of violence for religious reasons between Muslims and Christians. Both the Seljuk emperors and the Ilkhānid government were completely free of any feelings of religious fanaticism.[35] The Seljuk system of government in Anatolia was not at all of a theocratic nature. Although a theocratic government was required by the principles of Islamic law, the state placed its own interests and government—not in theory but in fact—above everything.

The development of urban life in Anatolia in the Seljuk period began, of course, in central and eastern Anatolia and then continued in western Anatolia. Consequently, up to the fourteenth century, there were no large cities in the west that could compare to those in, for example, central Anatolia. For political and economic reasons, the most important cities on the coasts of the Mediterranean and Black seas could not develop at a rate to rival the cities of the interior. Because the Seljuk state never possessed very large naval forces, centers of international trade like Sinop, Antalya and ʿAlāʾiyya were always vulnerable to raids by foreign fleets. Therefore, the exchange market {in these cities} had the character of a fortified quay protected by a strong garrison. Without the protection of a powerful naval force, it was impossible to ensure the development of commercial cities on the coasts. In addition, there were already large trading centers on the Mediterranean, like the port of Yumurtalık for Lesser Armenia, and on the Black Sea, like the port of Trebizond for the Empire of Trebizond, which were terminals on the major European-Asian commercial routes. They were more important than the Seljuk ports not only for transit trade but also for the foreign trade of Anatolia. It was natural that in this period, when internal trade in Anatolia and overland commerce with the Orient were more important, the *continental* centers would develop to a greater extent. It was only in the fourteenth century, when beyliks possessing important naval forces came into existence on the shores of the Mediterranean and Aegean seas, that urban life began in these maritime regions. But it is worthy of note that, politically, the most important cities of these beyliks developed not on the coasts but inland. It was also in the fourteenth century that urban life expanded in western Anatolia for reasons that are easy to understand.

Naturally, the development of trade and industry was the most fundamental factor in the development of urban life in Anatolia, as it was everywhere. One could admit that the increase in population density in some cities was due to political causes. However, if we look at the different cities, large and small, that existed throughout any country at a given time, we would feel the need to search for strictly economic reasons for increases in population. Because it is not possible to show here, one by one, the extent of the development of all the cities of Anatolia in the thirteenth century and the reasons for their development, let us just take Sivas as an example. This city, which is in the center of a rich agricultural area in the Kızıl Irmak Valley, has been geographically an important political and commercial center since the most ancient times. We can summarize the information given by all the sources that speak of this city in the thirteenth and fourteenth centuries in the following manner: Sivas was a large and flourishing city surrounded by a wall; it was known for the production of cereals, fruit, cotton, and textiles; it had 24 *khāns* {inns, warehouses}, a large cathedral mosque, neighborhood mosques, *madrasas* {Islamic "colleges" of law}, *tekkes* {dervish lodges}, palaces, and other beautiful buildings; its streets were large and its markets were crowded; merchants from Anatolia, Syria, al-Jazīra, and even from the West gathered there; its inhabitants were wealthy and addicted to ostentation and amusements; and it had a great many waqfs for the public good. Indeed, because its winters were so severe, there was even a waqf to provide food for birds when it snowed. Chalcocondyles states that the city had a population of 120,000 at that time. According to Qazvīnī, the people of the city were mostly Turkmen. This brief description suffices to show rather clearly the economic factors in the city's development. Although not as important as Sivas, Konya or Kayseri, there were a number of other cities in thirteenth century Anatolia—namely, Erzurum, Erzinjan, Harput, Amasya, Tokat, Niğde, Niksar, Kırshehir, Aksaray, Ankara, and so forth—the development of which can be attributed to the same economic factors.

Let me now briefly describe the internal life of these cities with a word about municipal organization in the commercial and industrial centers, which, exactly like Sivas, were inhabited mainly by Turks, and the social classes which arose from a sophisticated division of labor. Those who served the state or earned their living from the state treasury formed an important stratum of the urban population. Just as the functionaries of the central government constituted a rather large class in the capital, those in the local administration in the large cities also formed a rather large group. Whenever there was a prince in any of these cities, his *dīwān* {governing council} replicated on a smaller scale the staff of the dīwān of the central government, that is, of the great sultan. The palaces of the ruler and the princes, their principles of protocol, their manner of living, their receptions for ambassadors, their hunting parties, and their weddings were so magnificient and conspicuous that they are reminiscent of the courts at Baghdad and Constantinople, and the costs for this were enormous. The residences of the great military leaders and civilian notables and their manner of life were also very ostentatious and expensive.

The officials in the departments of state were compelled as well, according to their rank, to lead an extravagant way of life. All government positions were basically hereditary, not by law but by custom, and were filled by an aristocracy of bureaucrats from the families which had long been associated with, and had served, the ruling dynasty. In general, they possessed sufficient wealth to allow them to lead a luxurious life, corresponding to the importance of their positions. During Ilkhānid rule, a number of officials were appointed to Anatolia from other regions of the empire, but there was no real change in these conditions. In addition to their personal, that is, family, wealth, the class of civilian, judicial, and military officials also received important grants as compensation for their services. This class owned valuable property in the cities and extensive lands. Whenever it found an opportunity to use its accumulated funds as commercial capital, it invested in joint ventures with the great merchants and sometimes even made unscrupulous speculations, secretly of course.

Apart from government officials and the armed forces, religious scholars, teachers, preachers, shaikhs {elders, ṣūfī masters}, *seyyids* {descendants of the Prophet}, people attached to the court or the great notables, doctors, artisans, musicians, singers, in short, anyone who could find a way, under whatever title, received money from the state treasury. Furthermore, many hospitals, soup kitchens, madrasas, tekkes, and primary schools {*sıbyan mektepleri*} were built and operated thanks to the waqfs established by the rulers, members of the ruling family, male or female, the important and wealthy men of state, and the rich merchants. Although the social assistance, public education, and public works were very progressive for that time, they were not a burden on the state budget.

All these factors could be considered as causes for the development of the cities in thirteenth century Anatolia. It would be much more accurate, however, to regard them as results rather than causes. The largest block of urban population were the craftsmen who earned their living by manual labor. They were the major force that created the basis of city life, that filled the cities, and that was a counterweight {to the government}, sometimes by demonstrating moral discontent and sometimes by carrying out armed insurrection against administrative and fiscal corruption. It was basically commercial capital that ensured that these artisans were concentrated in the cities. In other words, although its numbers were small, it was the class of great merchants that controlled industrial activity. This enterprising class, which organized caravans to travel inside and outside the country and which provided goods from internal and external markets to satisfy city needs, managed not only its own capital but also the accumulated funds of the artisans, aristocratic families and bureaucrats, indeed, even the more moderate savings of the middle-class. It was the basic active element. In order to earn large profits, it had to accept great risks, hardships, and adventures. Urban industry, to some degree, tried to provide for the needs of the urban population and the villagers and nomads living around the cities. Frequent markets and fairs held at more lengthy intervals were arranged for this purpose.[36] Exchanges took place both in coin and in kind. But urban industry also attempted, to a certain extent, to produce the kinds of goods demanded by the entire internal market, and even the external market. Such factors as the availability of special basic materials in a city or its environs and the traditional longstanding concentration of the right kind of labor technology in a city were of fundamental importance in this regard.

Both the markets that were established for local needs, inside or outside the city, and the fairs that satisfied the need for a much wider exchange of goods were under the protection and control of the state. Indeed, the state received a certain tax from all transactions. It also had rather substantial military forces present at fairs in particular in order to protect them from raids by nomads or brigands.

3

LIFE ALONG THE BORDER AND THE FOUNDING OF THE OTTOMAN EMPIRE

I have shown what the political and social conditions were like in Anatolia when the Ottomans first appeared on the stage of history as a political entity, albeit a primitive and weak entity, in the northern corner of Anatolia. These general conditions must always be kept in mind in order to be able to understand the manner in which the Ottoman state was established. Furthermore, there are several other issues directly related to this great event that we need to understand. The first, which has been debated but not yet satisfactorily resolved, is that of ethnicity: What was the ethnic nature of the Turkish element that formed the original nucleus of the empire, that is, to which branch of the Turks did it belong? The solution to this controversial question will shed light on the second issue which has not yet been settled despite considerable debate, namely, the question of when this element came to Anatolia.

In my opinion, no matter how these two questions are solved, they are not of the utmost importance in explaining the manner in which the Ottoman state was established. Nevertheless, I will devote some space to them within the narrow framework of this lecture in order to describe the weakness of the theories that have been proposed on this subject and, above all, to show the meaninglessness of the great importance which, up to now, has been attributed to them. The task that will mainly occupy us here, however, is to describe the internal life on the marches, especially the western Anatolian marches, in the thirteenth and fourteenth centuries. This is extremely important in order for us to complete the description that was given in the last lecture on the social history of Anatolia and to understand not only the founding of the Ottoman state but also that of the other beyliks that took shape on the marches. After first understanding the social milieu in which this state appeared, it will be easier to explain the internal and external factors that quickly brought about the transformation of this small political entity into a powerful empire.

A. The Tribe of Osman

As for determining the origin of the Ottoman family itself, the early sources are unanimous in stating that the element which formed the nucleus of their state was, like the great majority of Turks who came to Anatolia with the Seljuks, the Oghuz, that is, the Turkmen. The opinion of some modern historians that this element belonged to another Turkish group named "Kanghlı" is not based on valid sources.[1]

While some sources are silent on the branch of the Oghuz to which this element belonged, others specify that it was the Qayı tribe. For example, in the anonymous books called *Tevārīh-i āl-i Osman*, which were popular works, in Shükrullah's *Behcet ül-tevārīh*, and in the histories of ʿĀshıq Pasha-Zāde and Uruj Bey, we are simply told that the Ottoman dynasty came from the Oghuz. On the other hand, in the *Saljūqnāme* of Yazıcıoğlu, who wrote during the reign of Murad II, it is specifically mentioned that the Ottomans were from the Qayı. This point is also made in certain traditions about the illustriousness and nobility of birth {*şerāfet ve asalet*} of the Qayı among the other Oghuz clans in genealogies like the *Jām-ı jem-āyīn*, in collections of native {*millī*} stories like those of *Dede Korkut*, in the histories of Rūhī, Lutfī Pasha, and Enverī's *Düstūrnāme*, and finally in Idrīs-i Bitlīsī's *Hesht bihisht*. We might also add that it has been generally accepted in works recently written in the East and

West that the Ottomans were from the Qayı tribe. The tradition that they were from the Oghuz is not, in fact, contrary to the tradition that they were from the Qayı. Furthermore, the tradition in favor of the Qayı is found in sources that are older than those previously mentioned. The fact that some of them were written when the Oghuz traditions had not yet been forgotten in Anatolia, indeed, the fact that legends about the illustriousness {*şeref*} and nobility of birth of the Qayı were fabricated, confirms this tradition. If the Ottoman rulers had not considered themselves to be from the Qayı, it would not have been necessary to fabricate such legends in the works written at their court. It might immediately come to mind that perhaps the Qayı were of special importance among the Oghuz clans and therefore it would have been natural for the Ottoman sultans to make such claims of nobility, but this was not the case. According to Oghuz tradition, the rulers were raised, above all, from the Salur or Qınıq clans. If the Ottoman sultans had wanted to falsify a genealogy for themselves, they would have considered themselves related to these clans. It is necessary to keep in mind that during the reign of Murad II, when this story about the Qayı was established, the old tribal traditions had not been entirely forgotten.[2] Specifically, it would have been meaningless to put forward a fabricated genealogy that was contrary to the traditions that were alive among the nomads.

Therefore, based on these observations, we can conclude that Osman, who founded the state and gave his name to it, and his father, Ertughrul, were at the head of an unimportant tribe—of no consequence in size—that belonged to the Qayı. There is no basis whatsoever to certain other views that have recently been asserted, such as that Osman was not Ertughrul's real son and that he was not nomadic but belonged to a settled element bound to orthodox Islam.[3] As for the genealogies which traced the Ottoman family back to the legendary forefather of the Turks, Oghuz Khān, they are similar to those found today in various forms among the Turkmen beyond the Caspian Sea. They were applied not only to the ruling family as has been thought, but also to the Qayı clan in general and were of purely legendary value.[4]

After the Ottoman state had become powerful, many family relationships of the ruling dynasty were also fabricated in order to enhance its nobility and, in this way, make it more attractive to certain elements within the empire. The various traditions that make Osman a member of the Comneni family[5] or trace his descent to the Prophet have, of course, no historical foundation at all. The only positive result that we can reach is that Osman's small tribe belonged to the Qayı.[6]

Although the great German scholar J. Marquart agreed that the Ottomans belonged to the Qayı, he vigorously asserted in an important work that these Qayı were not Turks but Mongols. Moreover, he tried to deduce from this a number of conclusions that would be inadmissible to a serious historian. He considered the Mongol tribe which had the name Qay and the Qayı—Qayığ in the old form—tribe to be one and the same.[7] While Professor Paul Pelliot stated in a review of Marquart's work, with his customary insight, that his conclusions on the problem of the Qayı were highly suspect,[8] some esteemed Turkologists like J. Németh and C. Brockelmann have accepted his opinion as fact.[9] In my book which appeared in 1918, I criticized this great error into which Marquart had fallen[10] and, in an article published in 1925, I described this problem in more detail.[11] The late Professor Barthold showed in some of his writings that he concurred with me on this point.[12]

As I mentioned above, the fact that the Ottomans were not of the Mongol race but belonged to the Qayı clan of the Oghuz was of no consequence at all to the historical march of events. The expectation of some philologists to reach certain conclusions from this with regard to linguistic history is not based on any solid foundation, for the small tribe in the company of Ertughrul and Osman was not a large block composed entirely of Oghuz Qayı. As I explained in the last lecture while discussing the migration that occurred in the Seljuk period, many of the Qayı who came to Anatolia with the Seljuks scattered to different areas of that region, indeed, perhaps more than the other clans. We know that during the history of the Anatolian Seljuks some Oghuz tribes carried out numerous movements and formed rather powerful blocks. Yet, neither before nor after the founding of the Ottoman state do we find any movement bearing the name of the Qayı. Given the paucity of the historical sources for Anatolia, we have to resort to other sources, especially toponomy {for information in this matter}. While not going into detail, let me briefly describe the results that I have obtained by doing so.

The Qayı, who, for a long time past, had been an important branch of the Oghuz, participated in the general movements of the Oghuz in the Seljuk period and went from the East toward the West. Some of them stopped and remained among the trans-Caspian Turkmen, some stayed in Māzandarān, Āzarbāījān or Arrān (southern Caucasus), and some mixed with other Turkish tribes. It is known that those who came to Anatolia divided into different groups and established themselves in widely scattered areas. Not only are there villages with the name Qayı in northern Anatolia—in the environs of Erzinjan and Sushehri, around Amasya, Chorum, Kastamonu, İlgaz, Chankırı, Gerede, Bolu, Düzce, and then in the regions of Eskishehir, Mihalich, and Orhan-eli—but the same village name is also clearly found in the south in the environs of Cilicia and around İsparta, Burdur and Fethiye and toward the west around Denizli, Muğla, Aydın and Ödemish. The aforesaid places indicate where the Qayı lived and show that they generally migrated toward the west.[13] Those members of the Qayı in the company of first Ertughrul and then of Osman were therefore a tiny fraction of the Qayı who had scattered to many places. Although they formed the nucleus of a new political entity, they had no effect whatsoever on the nature of the state that was created. A handful of people whose role was completely political, and determined somewhat by chance, they produced a state founder from among their ranks and initially served as his base of support, but it is impossible to attribute to them any other influence—as is sometimes done for example by claiming that they provided the basis of the "Ottoman dialect." In the event, we can say categorically that it would be historically impossible to distinguish this small part of a tribe from the other small Turkish tribes and Turks who lived on the marches of western Anatolia at that time and to attribute to it any unique characteristics or influence.

After thus establishing that the Ottomans were from the Qayı and that the Qayı had come to Anatolia with the first Seljuk conquerors and spread throughout the country, we can go on to an analysis and criticism of the complicated and contradictory traditions about the coming of the ancestors of the Ottoman dynasty to Anatolia. The older written sources generally state that the ancestors of the Ottomans came to eastern Anatolia with the Seljuks. In the later sources, it is recorded that they were living around Māhān in Khurāsān when they went to the west because of the invasion of Jenghiz Khān. Some writers combine both accounts, repeating that they first went to Khurāsān, then to Akhlat and from there continued further west. A number of European historians, from Hammer to Marquart and Gibbons, have attempted to reach some conclusions from these confusing reports of the annalists. All of these historians, and even the most recent works in the East and West that rely on them, continue to repeat that the Ottomans came to western Anatolia in the wake of the Mongol invasion. As I explained above, however, the tribe to which the Ottomans belonged, the Qayı, came to Anatolia after the initial Seljuk conquests and settled in numerous groups in many areas, especially on the marches. In light of this, it would seem that there is no historical basis to all the emigration stories that fill the old chronicles. Indeed, if the very nature of the early sources which provide these various accounts is taken into consideration and historical criticism is applied to the emigration stories, it would be impossible not to reach this conclusion. Fortunately, as I mentioned above, these are not questions of fundamental importance for understanding the founding of the Ottoman Empire.

Let me briefly summarize the positive results of all this. At the end of the thirteenth century, Ertughrul and then

Osman were chiefs of a small tribe belonging to the Qayı. It was one of the tribes on the marches which were subject in theory, but not in fact, to the sultans in Konya and later to the Ilkhānids. This tribe lived in the Turco-Byzantine border area around Eskishehir in northwestern Phrygia. There were at that time, however, numerous march beys who lived on the frontiers of western Anatolia. They attacked and plundered Byzantine territory whenever they found an opportunity and even captured certain fortifications and towns and laid the foundation for new political entities. How and why was Osman, who was at the head of a small and insignificant tribe, able to establish the basis of a new political entity like the Ottoman state in such an area and among many rival powers? In order to be able to answer this, we need to understand, above all, the internal life on the marches, namely, the social conditions and the religious, economic, and political factors at work there.

B. Life on the Marches

1. Military and Administrative Organization

As a result of their continuous struggles with Byzantium, the Umayyad and ʿAbbāsid empires established a special military and administrative system along the frontiers. The Anatolian Seljuks created a similar system on the eastern and western borders of their own country. This frontier organization, which was established on the one hand for defense against enemy attacks, and on the other, for seizing any opportunity to raid and capture booty from the territory of the enemy, naturally relied on the Turkmen tribes. In fact, because of this, first E. Quatremère,[14] and then Barbier de Meynard,[15] Stanislas Guyard,[16] Ch. Schefer,[17] E. Blochet,[18] R. Nicholson, and Huart,[19] believed that the word *uc* {meaning "march"} that they encountered in numerous Muslim texts was the name of a Turkish tribe, a misconception that I tried to dispel in one of my articles.[20] One of the more important march organizations of the Seljuk state in the thirteenth century was along the Mediterranean shore, including the border with Lesser Armenia and such ports as Antalya and ʿAlāʾiyya. But the most important was on the border with the Empire of Nicaea in western Anatolia. In order to protect its maritime regions, the Seljuk state assigned commanders, and beys who were under their authority, to the coasts of the Mediterrranean and Black seas. But the land borders were more important.

When they thought it was necessary, the sultans reinforced their armies with forces that they called up from the marches. These forces were composed of nomadic Turkmen tribes led by their own chiefs. The central government gave the title of "march bey" {*uc beyi*} to some tribal chiefs who had acquired power by various means and had brought numerous small tribes under their control. Above them, however, one or more great march emīrs {*uc emīri*} were appointed from among the high state officials. We learn from the historical sources that in the thirteenth century the central government appointed great emīrs like the Yaghıbasanids, Ali Bey, and the Ṣāḥib Atāids, that there existed a number of great march beys like Ghāzī Mehmed Bey, Salur Bey, and İlyas Bey, and that sometimes they were strong enough to oppose the government and cause it major difficulties. The march beys paid a certain tribute in cash and kind to the state treasury and they would visit the capital for many reasons, sometimes to settle their accounts. Ghāzī Mehmed Bey, who seems to have had great influence over the large tribes in such coastal areas as Antalya and ʿAlāʾiyya, and along the Menderes River on the southwestern Seljuk border, invented a white conical hat for the military forces on the marches in order to distinguish them from the Turkmen who generally wore red conical hats.[21] I believe that it would not be a mistake to trace back to Ghāzī Mehmed the origin of the "white headgear of the akhīs" mentioned by Ibn Baṭṭūṭa, and the white headgear (*ak börk*) that the Ottoman ruler Orhan and those in his company wore—on the origin of which all kinds of strange theories have recently been proposed.

There are many questions about which we can say nothing definite, such as the method of administering the marches and their relationship to the central government. We only know that the Turkmen on the marches who were not yet subject to the central government in the twelfth century carried out operations against the Byzantines on their own. They launched raids and captured enormous booty and thousands of prisoners. These prisoners, who were either set free in exchange for ransom or were sold, as was the case throughout the medieval world, assured them a significant material profit. Sometimes a very high ransom was obtained for these prisoners because of their political and social status. The independent actions of these powerful Turkmen tribes, which, much more than the disciplined Seljuk forces, harassed the army of Frederick Barbarosa as it passed through Anatolia and, in the time of the Comneni, advanced as far as the environs of Edremid in search of pastures for their herds, caused certain difficulties in the foreign policy of the Seljuk emperors and sometimes forced them into a war with Byzantium against their wishes.[22] According to the contemporary custom of warfare, however, local clashes and raids on the marches never violated the peace between states if one of the two sides did not wish to use this as a pretext {for full-scale war}.[23] Although the Empire of Nicaea had good relations with the sultanate at Konya, it took defensive measures on the frontier in order to protect its territory from continuous Turkmen raids. Even during the time of the Arab invasions, a defensive line composed of fortified positions at militarily important points, especially at mountain passes, was built along the border and detachments of border guards called *akritai* were raised to defend this line. This method of defending the border, which had originally been quite strong, was subject to different changes over the centuries and gradually weakened.

This border system, which was re-established toward the west at the time of the Seljuk Empire and was completely reorganized in the second half of the twelfth century under the Comneni,[24] was concentrated in the mountains of Bithynia, that is, in the northwestern corner of Asia Minor, in the thirteenth century. The border guards, who were called *kharā'iṭa*, i.e., akritai, in the Muslim sources, possessed certain lands and were exempt from taxes. During the time of the Empire of Nicaea, they successfully carried out their duties. After the capital was transferred to Constantinople, this defensive organization was long neglected. Indeed, in order to secure additional income for the treasury of the empire, whose expenses were increasing daily, Michael VIII Palaeologus confiscated a considerable portion of the lands whose revenues belonged to the akritai. In reaction to this loss of economic support, they rebelled, but were severely punished.[25] One might guess that many of these border guards, who belonged to different elements, went over to the other side—like, for example, the Christian Cuman Turks, ten thousand families of whom were transferred from Rumelia by Emperor {John III Ducas} Vatatzes in the first half of the thirteenth century and established along this border.[26] The weakening of the Byzantine border defenses after the capital was moved from Nicaea had a major effect on, and greatly facilitated, the slow but sure expansion toward the west of the territories of the Turkish beys on the marches and the founding of new political entities on the Byzantine border when Seljuk authority weakened under Mongol pressure.

Although the beys of the Turkish tribes on the marches were formally subject to the Seljuk sultanate, they did not hesitate to carry out independent operations, without paying attention to it, whenever they found an opportunity. They usually paid taxes only as the result of actual threats. In the struggles for the throne among the Seljuk princes, they would take the side of one of them and add to the internal strife. In every insurrection, the rebels took refuge with the march beys or received definite help from the march tribes. When the central government weakened, even the caravans of the wealthy Turkish merchants within the country were exposed to raids by these tribes. Up to the time of Baybars' occupation of Kayseri, that is, while the

Mongols did not yet have de facto control of Anatolia, these march beys did not recognize the central government and military forces had to be dispatched against them. They later took an even more hostile position toward Ilkhānid rule and, by taking advantage of the internal administrative confusion, strengthened their local influence. The family of Ṣāḥib Atā, who was appointed emīr of the marches during the government of Muʿīn al-Dīn Pervāne, that is, before Abaqa came to Anatolia to take revenge for {the support given to} Baybars' invasion, was given Kütahya, Sandıklı, Gorgorom, and Akshehir as *khāṣṣ* {part of the royal domain}. At the beginning of the fourteenth century, first Emīr Choban and then his son Demirtash, the Ilkhānid governor, were able to establish their power on these marches by taking various political measures or carrying out punitive military operations according to the situation and acknowledging the de facto existence of the beyliks on the marches as "subject states." In one source from around the middle of the fourteenth century, {the lands of the} Qaramānids, Germiyānids, Ḥamīdids, İnānjids, Orhan, and Umur Bey, {as well as} Sinop, Kastamonu, Gerede, and Bolu are described as the countries on the Anatolian marches which were subject to the Ilkhānids and paid taxes to them.[27] Certain coins and inscriptions, and a reference in {Ibn Faḍl Allāh al-ʿUmarī's} *Masālik al-abṣār*, give the impression that, even around the time of the final decline and fall of the Ilkhānid state, Mongol rule had not completely disappeared from these states on the marches. This was probably the result of their policy of maintaining good relations with the powerful state of Eretna which was the successor of Ilkhānid rule in Anatolia.

The marches were not simply regions containing summer and winter pastures reserved for the nomadic or seminomadic Turkmen tribes. In addition to the summer and winter pastures reserved for each tribe, there were also a great many villages, small towns, and even small fortified positions at strategic points. Furthermore, somewhat behind the border were some rather large, but not very numerous, cities. These well-defended cities which had been captured from the Byzantines served as the capitals of the march beyliks. And just as there were both Christian villages and Muslim villages in the Turkish area, the population of the cities was also a mixture of Christians and Muslims. Conversely, one could also find Muslim Turks settled in Byzantine territory.

2. The Population: Ethnic and Religious Elements

Land was divided into *timars* {an allotment, for a specific period, of a portion of revenue from land} of different values. Timars producing a small income were set aside for march soldiers who held the title of *ghāzī* {warrior for the faith}, according to Muslim tradition, or *alp* {hero} according to Turkish tradition. They were usually hereditary and were transferred from father to son.[28] In addition to the Turks who had completely taken up an agricultural life, there were also on the marches a number of adventurers who had come from throughout the Turco-Islamic world in search of a livelihood for themselves by any means, and Turks who had left central Anatolia because of the pressure from the Mongols and searched for land or pastures where they could establish themselves with their families and herds. The people under Byzantine rule who had suffered from a lack of security or heavy taxation within Byzantine territory preferred to come under the administration of the Turkish beyliks which provided security for life and property in return for light taxes. This was better than remaining subject to Byzantium, which was satisfied with collecting taxes without providing any security.[29] This situation occurred, however, only after these march beyliks, which had slowly evolved from tribes that lived by raiding, had begun to develop into well-organized political entities that protected the interests of their subjects. The political and administrative anarchy resulting from Byzantine dynastic quarrels, military weakness, the cruelties committed against the people by bands of adventurer mercenaries like the Catalans, whose assistance had been requested, and hostility against the Latins and Catholicism, all contributed to the continuous advance of the Turkish border toward the west. Meanwhile, the arrival of madrasa graduates from the major Muslim cities in Iran, Egypt, and the Crimea and members of the Seljuk and Ilkhānid bureaucracies from central and eastern Anatolia slowly led to the creation of cultural institutions in the march beyliks and the establishment of administrative mechanisms. As the marches advanced, the life in the villages and cities behind them flourished, the population increased, and economic activity expanded.

Because these march areas were on the confines of the *dār al-islām* {abode of Islam}, this gave a more or less religious nature, and an aura of a *holy war*, to the struggles that took place there. This in turn attracted all kinds of people possessing different religious creeds wrapped in the garb of the warrior-dervish, as well as vagabond dervish groups, all of whom apparently came to fight for Islam but, in fact, were seeking a means of livelihood. As I will discuss shortly, some of them were Turkmen dervishes who went among the villages and nomads spreading an effective heterodox propaganda. They even propagandized the Christians. On the other hand, many of the dervishes who settled in the cities and towns belonged to the completely different Sunnī brotherhoods and were never able to exercise a strong influence on the Turkmen tribes. Despite the propaganda of both the dervish brotherhoods that took root in the cities and the madrasas, we encounter no conflict for religious reasons between the Muslim and Christian elements which lived under the same rule on the marches. We can go even further and apply this, without hesitation, as an axiom to the history of Anatolia in the late Middle Ages and especially to the history of the Seljuk period. I briefly touched on this question above while describing life in the cities. Certain actions like the attempt, for a while, by Demirtash, who pursued an extremist Islamic policy in Anatolia and wanted to play the role of mahdī, to distinguish Christians and Jews by their clothing were short-lived, very rare, and prove nothing. Moreover, we possess considerable evidence to show that the Seljuk emperors and Dānishmendids had long had a liberal and egalitarian policy toward both their Muslim and Christian subjects.[30]

Although Muslim and Christian elements lived on the border of two mutually hostile states, those of the Turks and Byzantium, no really intense hostility existed between them. Even before the middle of the twelfth century, Byzantine historians report that the Greeks who lived on the islets in Lake Beyshehir, which was then in the border region, adopted the customs and habits of the Turks because of their close relations with them. Indeed, as a result of friendly relations with the Turks, they paid no attention to the orders of the Byzantine emperor.[31] F. Chalandon has quite rightly emphasized the significance of this occurrence to show very clearly the nature of Muslim-Christian relations on the marches. Henri Grégoire, who has published very important studies in recent years on the epic of Digenis Akritas and the story of Seyyid Battāl, has quite correctly shown that these works are not the expression of two hostile societies separated from each other by an unbridgeable religious gulf but, to the contrary, they are a reflection of two social groups, living under similar conditions, which were in continuous, close, and even friendly contact with each other.[32] One can also see this in another Turkish story, namely, the *Dānishmendnāme*, which is nothing but a continuation of the story of Seyyid Battāl, and in the book of *Dede Korkut*, which contains some scenes of the struggles of the Ak-Koyunlu Turkmen against the Empire of Trebizond. Despite the scenes of struggle, in which there are characters of epic proportions and sentiments of religious fanaticism, one does not sense a deep feeling of hostility in any of this. It is well-known of course that there was fighting between Turkish and Byzantine forces on the borders in the thirteenth and fourteenth centuries and that some conquests were exhausting and bloody for both sides. Furthermore, there are sources which show that the people in the cities and country fled in panic in the wake of a defeated army. Yet, in spite of all such events, which were very natural for that period, the mutual state of affairs of the Muslims and Christians, even on the hostile marches, was as I have described above.

3. Islamization

Let me briefly discuss here, in passing, the question of conversion to Islam. To be sure, there were Christians in Anatolia who converted to Islam in the Seljuk period. In fact, we know that among the Seljuk notables there were a number of converts related to the upper Byzantine aristocracy, even to the Comneni family. In addition, there were, among the scholars, artisans, and even famous mystics, converts or the sons of converts from Christianity. Long contact, the privileged position of Muslims in the state government, and the desire to be free of certain taxes which were imposed on non-Muslims, in short, psychological and economic factors were both at work to some degree in this matter.

We know of course that, at the time of the Ilkhānids, pressures of a religious nature were sometimes applied against the Muslims. Indeed, Baydu favored the Christians and, with their encouragement, took certain measures against the Muslims. But we should not forget that such actions—carried out much more for political than religious purposes—were of limited duration. Although we know that, even in the second half of the fourteenth century, some Mongol notables in Anatolia had still not become Muslims, it is certain that the Muslim element in Anatolia regained its former privileged position, beginning in particular with the reign of Ghāzān. Nevertheless, even under these circumstances, we can say that the conversion of Christians in eastern and central Anatolia in the Seljuk and Ilkhānid periods was not as extensive as has been claimed. This is confirmed by al-Aqsarāyī's statement that the *jizya* {head tax on non-Muslims} collected from the Anatolian Christians at the end of the thirteenth century was a significant portion of the general revenue.

One wonders how extensive conversion was in the territories of the Turkish beyliks in western Anatolia in the fourteenth century? Did a large proportion of the Greeks, especially in the Ottoman area, convert as a number of leading Byzantinists and many historians, including Gibbons, have claimed? In order to support this theory, Gibbons gives Bursa and especially Nicaea as examples. The famous declaration that the Byzantine patriarchate addressed to the people of Nicaea in 1339–40 does, of course, indicate that rather widespread conversion was taking place there. One should not, however, read more into this than it states. Under Byzantine rule, Nicaea had been a very prosperous city. But according to the testimony of Ibn Baṭṭūṭa, who passed through it shortly after it fell to the Turks, "it possessed a very small population." We cannot explain this small population, as Gibbons does, by the conversion of a large part of its people and their dispersion throughout Ottoman territory. After the capital of the empire was moved to Constantinople, the area around Nicaea became part of an insecure border country and thus the population of the city must have declined considerably long before the Ottomans conquered it. Moreover, if all the people in the city had converted, Orhan would certainly have left them alone. In addition, it must be kept in mind that the Ottoman state never followed a "policy of Islamization" and that the wholsale conversion of the great cities was generally impossible.[33]

Although Ottoman sources, for example ʿĀshıq Pasha-Zāde, state that during the initial Ottoman conquests some Christian villages completely converted to Islam because of the justice of the Ottoman government, such stories based on oral traditions are of doubtful historical value. Indeed, ʿĀshıq Pasha-Zāde says nothing about conversion in the cities and even states that the Christians in the conquered areas kept their religion. According to Ottoman sources, Göynük, which was completely inhabited by Christians when Ibn Baṭṭūṭa passed through it, should have been Islamized toward the end of the same century, since Yıldırım Bayezid {i.e., Bayezid I} had people brought from there and from Torbalı to establish the Muslim quarter that he founded in Constantinople. Even if this report were true, it would be more correct to explain it by the establishment of a new Turkish element there than by a general conversion. Logically one cannot easily accept that the Muslim quarter in Constantinople was simply settled by Greeks who had recently become Muslims. Official documents prove that, in areas that Gibbons claims were immediately Islamized, there were villages exclusively inhabited by Greeks during the reign of Mehmed I, and even Murad II {Mehmed II in Fr. ed.}. In light of all this evidence, it would be more correct and more prudent not to imagine that there was "mass conversion that occurred quickly" in either the Ottoman beylik or others in western Anatolia.

As will be readily apparent from the description that I have given above, these march beyliks were in a position to increase their population continuously thanks to the Turkish and Muslim elements that arrived from the east. Consequently, there is no need whatsoever to assert, as Gibbons does, that conversion was a factor in the increase in Muslim population. My remarks are not meant to catagorically deny that some Christian elements became Muslim in the first half {second half in Fr. ed.} of the fourteenth century. The status of the Orthodox Church, which had lost its moral prestige among the masses as early as the twelfth century, created a state of mind that excused such conversion, especially when confronted with economic advantages. For heterodox groups, conversion was even easier. Regarding this matter, I would only like to point out here that conversion in Anatolia at that time was relatively limited and slow. In the Ottoman Empire conversion on a large scale occurred only after the Ottoman state was established in the Balkans. It took place in that region in the fifteenth century in particular and continued in the sixteenth and seventeenth centuries. It will therefore be clear from what I have described that the claim that the Ottomans "needed the Greek converts in order to obtain administrators while establishing their initial political system" is completely baseless. Today it is a historical fact that all the great statesmen of the fourteenth century were Turks, that even Evrenos (*Evren* + *uz*),[34] who was alleged to have been a Greek convert, was a member of the old Turkish aristocracy, and that only a few people from among the leading personalities were converts.

The Ottoman state was founded exclusively by Turks in the fourteenth century. It was after this state began to develop into a great empire ruling various elements—after the first half of the fifteenth century—that, as occurred with the Byzantine and ʿAbbāsid empires, other elements, which in this case were "Ottomanized," entered the government. Moreover, just as the fact that a significant number of the rulers of the Byzantine Empire came from foreign elements is no proof that the Greeks lacked administrative ability, an analogous situation occurring in the Ottoman Empire cannot be used as proof that the Turks lacked administrative ability.

4. Military, Religious, and Corporative Associations

After describing the conditions of social life and the mutual state of affairs of the Turkish and Christian elements in the march beyliks, let me try to present one by one, and in the most general terms, the different social organizations that were active in those areas. ʿĀshıq Pash-Zāde, one of the first Ottoman annalists, mentions in one place in his work the existence of four large independent organizations which must be understood in order to get a clear idea of the political and social history of the march beyliks as well as of Anatolia in general. One must search for their roots in the early centuries of medieval Islamic history and in many geographic areas of the Muslim world. These social groups appeared under different names at various times and places and came to resemble each other and very often even merged with each other. The information provided on these organizations in the most fundamental sources, many of which are still in manuscript and are poorly known even to specialists, is vague, subject to numerous interpretations, or mistaken. Consequently, no sound and positive conclusions have been reached on this subject to date. Because I have done research for a long time on these kinds of social groups in the Muslim world, I would like to present here, in the briefest and simplest form, the results of my work.

a. GHĀZĪS and *ALPS*. This group, which ʿĀshıq Pasha-Zāde calls *ghāziyān-ı rūm* and other sources call by such titles as *alps* and *alp-erens*, was a social organization that existed not only at the time of the *collapse* of the empire of the Anatolian Seljuks, but also during the very first conquests in Anatolia. Among the pre-Islamic Turks, alp was a title having the meaning of "hero, warlike" and was given to princes.[35] It continued to be used after the Turks became Muslims and, in fact, was one of the official titles used in the Muslim Turkish states. Nevertheless, after the Turks embraced Islam, they began to use the title *ghāzī*, sometimes coupled with alp and sometimes alone in a religious sense. It appears that this honorary title, which was given to champions of the faith, was used as a title in Anatolia by the Dānishmendid family and later by a number of rulers of the march beyliks. One rarely encounters the title alp among the leading figures of the Anatolian Seljuks, who held many titles reserved for the military commanders {*ümera*} of the Muslim states, but it was very common among the military commanders of the march beyliks.

The term ghāzī, which was sometimes used in the historical sources for the individual soldiers of the Muslim armies in general, usually had a narrower and more specific meaning, namely, a certain group in the army or large cities.[36] We know that this ghāzī group, which existed in the armies of the Anatolian Seljuks, the Dānishmendids, and even before that of the Great Seljuks, was also found much earlier at the time of the Sāmānids in the regions of Khurāsān and Transoxiana.[37] It was quite natural for there to come into existence such a parasitic class, which, generally possessing no lands on which to live nor gainful employment, sought, in the face of economic necessity, a means of livelihood in the continuous wars and intestinal turmoil of the Middle Ages. The narrow basis and weakness of the system of government and the frequent need for rulers and commanders {*emirler*} to find mercenary soldiers to use against foreign and domestic enemies resulted in the establishment of such groups on the borders as well as in the large political and cultural centers. We know that an organization called the ghāzīs existed in Transoxiana in the tenth century and that it very closely resembled the organization of the *ʿayyārs* which, around the end of the eighth century, took advantage of the internal struggles of the ʿAbbāsid dynasty to become powerful in Baghdad, and in the first half of the eleventh century intercepted revenue for that city and collected taxes for its own benefit.[38] In the ninth century, during the time of the Ṭāhirids and Ṣaffārids, there existed in Iran similar organizations, again having the same names. In the Sāmānid period, the ghāzīs in Transoxiana were so called because they fought a holy war on the borders against unbelievers, that is, against the pagan Turks, and this was a title connoting religious pride.[39] Because of their numerical significance, their organization was officially recognized by the state. While one contemporary annalist, Baihaqī, mentions their chiefs having the title *sipāhsālār-ı gāzīyān*, the contemporary historian al-ʿUṭbī uses the name *raʾīs al-fityān* for them and another contemporary historian, Gardīzī, describes the same men as *ʿayyārların başı* {head of the ʿayyārs}. None of these writers who mention the same organization under three separate names are mistaken in their nomenclature, for these names were used synonomously from the earliest times.

With evidence from various sources—not only historical, but also ṣūfī and literary—belonging to the ʿAbbāsid period, I can further clarify this matter, concerning which the late Professor Barthold was the first to draw serious attention.[40] Al-Ṭabarī cites some poetry belonging to around the beginning of the ninth century which shows that the word *fatā* {youth, hero} was used to describe the ʿayyārs.[41] Ibn al-Athīr, while mentioning the great disorders in Baghdad caused by groups of people of every kind who came from everywhere in response to the call for *ghazā* {conquest, holy war} (361 A.H./971–72 A.D.), describes these groups as ʿayyār, *fityān*, and *nubuwwiyya*. The Arab traveler Ibn Jubayr also mentions this last group and states that it existed in Syria in the twelfth century.[42] But Ibn al-Athīr's reference tells us that it already existed two centuries earlier. Ibn Kathīr (473 A.H./1080–81 A.D.) says that the fityān existed as a well-organized group in Baghdad. Similar living conditions in the major industrial and commercial centers probably gave rise to this social class from the very earliest times. This class, whose name, costume, and ethical principles changed to some degree according to time and place, and whose members participated in brigandage, robbery, and bullying in the large cities whenever there was an opportunity, served as volunteers or mercenaries in domestic struggles or on the frontiers, belonged to the guild organizations and so were bound to them, and undermined the social order of the large cities during times of unemployment or when conditions permitted. This class was always present in Transoxiana, Khurāsān, Iran, Iraq, Syria, North Africa, and Anatolia, both before and after the Mongol invasion, under the names *ḥarāfisha, ʿayyārān, shaṭṭārān, mutaṭawwiʿa, juʿaydiyya, zanāṭira,* fityān or *futuwwatdārān, runūd* and others. In order to explain the distinct changes in meaning that these names and related expressions underwent and the differences among them, it would be necessary to describe the historical evolution of these groups. This would have to be the subject of a long and completely separate study.

The important group known in the history of Islamic mysticism as the "Malāmatiyya of Khurāsān" was related in certain ways to the ʿayyār organization in Khurāsān.[43] Thus, a number of special ṣūfī words—*muruwwa*, futuwwa, etc.—were used in the terminology of both groups, although the meanings they expressed were somewhat different. When corporations were established according to the various professions in the major industrial and commercial centers of the Islamic world, words like these also entered their terminology because they had ties to both the ṣūfī groups and the ʿayyārs and associations similar to them. Indeed, the same influences are fairly evident in the formation and development of the ethical principles that were particular to the corporations.

Massignon is quite right in defining the term futuwwa to mean *chevalerie insurrectionelle, héroisme hors lois*, although this term naturally took on a somewhat different spiritual meaning among the ṣūfī brotherhoods. But for the social class that I am discussing, futuwwa, having the primary meaning of heroism, was used as an ethical principle. This principle was not adopted by the ʿayyārs and similar organizations in 535 A.H./1140 A.D. as Massignon states,[44] but must be traced back at least another three hundred years. As I mentioned a little earlier, the famous ʿAbbāsid caliph al-Nāṣir attempted to bring under his own authority the futuwwa groups that were in areas where the moral power of the caliphate had some influence in order to both increase his prestige and find a source of support for himself. Many Muslim rulers were inducted into this organization by this caliph. Al-Nāṣir, who had belonged to the futuwwa organization for some time and wore the *shalvar* {baggy trousers} associated with its members, believed that the Near Eastern Islamic world, which may have had some contact with Western chivalry, would welcome his effort in this undertaking, and his belief proved to be well-founded. In this way, the ʿAbbāsid caliph rescued the futuwwa organization from being "an assembly of vagabonds" and gave it a guise of legitimacy. By introducing members of the highest aristocracy to this organization, he created a form of Muslim chivalry having high ethical values as well as social status. It is equally obvious that the caliph wanted to "create a new social force that was morally bound to his person" in response to the spread of ṣūfī brotherhoods throughout the Muslim world. These brotherhoods were formally under the state's control but never recognized its moral authority.[45] After conquering Sinop, the Seljuk emperor ʿIzz al-Dīn Kai-Kāʾūs I sent shaikh Majd al-Dīn Isḥāqī to the caliph, along with a great many gifts, and informed him that he wanted to join this organization. His wish was granted and a futuwwa shalvar was sent to him.[46]

In Anatolia in the thirteenth and fourteenth centuries, one encounters the title ghāzī primarily in the names of the march beys, but there is no reference to any organization under this name in either the cities of central Anatolia or on the marches. Indeed, in place of this name, which is found in Ottoman sources from the fifteenth and sixteenth centuries (in such expressions as ghāziyān-ı rūm in ʿĀshıq Pasha-Zāde), is the term alp. The early Ottoman sources add the title alp to the names of a great many commanders in the company of Osman Ghāzī. The well-known Turkish poet ʿĀshıq Pasha {ʿĀshıq Pasha-Zāde was his great grandson}, who lived in the first half of the fourteenth century, says that in order to become an alp or—to give a ṣūfī quality to this proud title which came from Turkish tradition—alp-eren, one had to fulfill nine conditions: "be strong-hearted, that is, brave, be strong-armed, zealous, have a good horse, special clothing, a bow, a good sword, a lance, and a suitable companion."[47] It therefore appears that the organization of alps on the marches of western Anatolia at that time, an organization that was especially associated with old Turkish traditions, was different from the organization of ghāzīs which, as I mentioned above, was more of a city organization and was based on Islamic traditions. It was quite natural for it to be found among the tribes of semi-nomadic Turkmen who constituted the primary military force of the march beyliks and whose native traditions had not been corrupted. As for the march beys who took the title ghāzī, they did so because they had adopted city life and had more or less come under the influence of the madrasas. Thus, the group that ʿĀshıq Pasha-Zāde wanted to describe under the name ghāziyān-ı rūm, the nature of which he did not understand very well, was undoubtedly that of the alps. It is true that Shāh Ismāʿīl, the founder of the Ṣafavid Empire in the sixteenth century, calls the Turkmen warriors who formed his army and considered him to be not only a political and military chief but also a religious leader, or more correctly a *murshid* {spiritual guide}, ghāzīs or ṣūfīs but not alps. This was the result, however, of a long religious evolution of two centuries.

b. AKHĪS. The second group whose importance in Anatolia is mentioned by ʿĀshıq Pasha-Zāde is the *akhīyān-ı rūm*, that is, the akhīs of Anatolia. Thanks to the testimony of Ibn Baṭṭūṭa, the extent to which this association had spread in Anatolia in the fourteenth century has long been known. The question of the role of the akhīs in the founding of the Ottoman state has therefore attracted attention for some time. Some light has been shed on the nature of this organization as a result of the studies that Orientalists have published on it for the past fifteen years and the new research that has been done on a number of *futuwwatnāmes* from various periods. But from the historical point of view, the obscurity surrounding this matter has still not been removed.[48]

Ibn Baṭṭūṭa especially mentions the lodges of this group, to which he gives the name *akhīyyat al-fityān* ("brotherhood of brave men"), in the main centers of Anatolia—Antalya, Burdur, Gölhisar, Ladik, Milas, Barjın, Konya, Niğde, Aksaray, Kayseri, Sivas, Gümüsh, Erzinjan, Erzurum, Birgi, Tire, Manisa, Balıkesir, Bursa, Gerede, Geyve, Yenije, Mudurnu, Bolu, Kastamonu, Sinop—but he also says they were found in every Turkmen town and village in Anatolia. In fact, toponymic analysis, as well as inscriptions, tombstones, waqf documents, official records, and finally numerous historical sources, show that this organization had spread throughout Anatolia, and even to Āzarbāījān and the coastal cities of the Crimea, all of which had close relations with Anatolia. This situation also pertained to the thirteenth century, especially the second half, although perhaps not to the same extent and level of development. In works from the Seljuk period in which the events in some of the large cities are described, one finds references to both the runūd and *akhīyān* as a powerful social organization, that is, to members of the *rinds* and akhīs or the futuwwa. Among these terms, which are synonymous, the word rind (pl. runūd) is found having exactly the same meaning as ʿayyār in sources from previous centuries and from different regions. This group, which was especially strong in the big cities and by its very nature was an urban organization, represented none other than the same entities that I mentioned above, the ʿayyārs, shāṭṭārs, ghāzīs, and so forth. ʿĀshıq Pasha-Zāde, who was a very simple and uneducated man, describes this association and the ghāzīs as being separate from each other, but he is completely deceived by these terms. He certainly would have been more correct if he had distinguished the alps and akhīs from each other.[49]

In any event, the akhī organization was found not only in the cities but also in the villages and on the marches to the extent that it had made contact with the organization of the alps and had infiltrated it. Indeed, one comes across persons who were called both alp and akhī, that is, they belonged to both groups at the same time. In like manner, the guild corporations and the futuwwa organization in the great cities subsequently merged with each other, the futuwwa organization becoming powerful above all in the big cities of Anatolia. During important ceremonies and the festivities welcoming the new ruler to a city, its members were present with their special music, banners, and costumes and were fully armed. We know that in the large cities they formed different groups under different chiefs and each group had its own meeting lodge. We can infer from this that probably every group and lodge was restricted to the members of a different trade. If the members of a trade in a large city were too numerous to meet in one lodge, they opened additional lodges in other parts of the city. This seems to have been the case from a report by Aflākī who says that akhī Aḥmad Shāh, who was chief of the akhīs in Konya in the second half of the thirteenth century, had several thousand rinds under his authority. It also appears in the same source that there were sometimes violent rivalries between the chiefs in a city. These rivalries perhaps came about for personal reasons or because of the conflicting economic interests of two persons or two groups. In any case, as I stated above, it appears that this social organization participated in, or influenced, a great many important historical events that took place in the cities of Anatolia in the thirteenth century. It would be worth a special study to show how the akhīs always joined movements that were against the central government. For example, they united with the Qaramānids when they rose against the Seljuk government in a rebellion that succeeded in giving them temporary control of Konya. During one of their temporary occupations of that city, however, in the period of the Ilkhānid governors, the Qaramānids hanged the chief of the akhīs.

Ibn Baṭṭūṭa says that this futuwwa organization was composed of groups of unmarried youths who were led by a chief, with the title akhī, who was chosen from among them. Yet, inscriptions, tombstones, waqf documents, in short, every kind of historical source shows that the akhīs, that is, the men in charge of this organization, were not just young unmarried workers as Ibn Baṭṭūṭa states. It is known that they included married men, men who had won the respect of the great emīrs, indeed, of the rulers, men of great wealth and influence, and men who held high government positions. During times when the state government broke down and anarchy ensued, that is, during periods of transition, the akhīs, namely, the chiefs of the futuwwa, who had the support of their organization, took control of the administration of the cities and tried to prevent the passage from the old to the new government from causing a major disruption. The power and influence that such an organization acquired, especially during periods of anarchy, is obvious. At those times when the system of government was not effective, it was the members of this organization who, in the small towns, represented not the power of the state but the local popular administration, which was more important.

It is highly likely that, after ʿIzz al-Dīn Kai-Kāʾūs I joined the futuwwa, this organization became more powerful in the cities of Anatolia and, in conformity with the general tendency of the period and the intellectual currents within the spiritual milieu of Anatolia, acquired a ṣūfī tint. On the one hand, the futuwwa penetrated the corporations and invigorated them while gaining strength for itself. On the other, it spread to the villages and made contact with the alp organization, that is, the landowning *sipāhīs* {"cavalrymen"}. From the second half of the thirteenth century to the fourteenth century {fifteenth century in Fr. ed.}, we find a considerable number of great statesmen, judges, *mudarrises* {professors of law in the madrasas}, shaikhs of different brotherhoods, and leading merchants in the futuwwa organization in Anatolia. This is a sign of the growing social importance of this organization. The penetration of the principles of the futuwwa, thus reinforced, of the guild corporations, that is, the reorganization of the corporations within the framework of the futuwwa, must have occurred in Anatolia after the first quarter of the thirteenth century. I believe this can be deduced from an analysis of all the historical sources and the various futuwwatnāmes that were written in different centuries in Anatolia. As I previously stated, the fact that, at the beginning of the fourteenth century, young unmarried workers in the large cities usually belonged to akhī lodges misled a great many researchers; some scholars considered this organization to be a guild organization while others thought it to be a futuwwa brotherhood comparable to the ṣūfī brotherhoods. However, there never existed in the Islamic world a brotherhood called a futuwwa brotherhood and the akhīs in Anatolia were not simply a guild organization. Furthermore, the fact that the word futuwwa was commonly used as an "ethical principle" among the ṣūfīs, ʿayyārs, and guild corporations has misled some of the medieval Oriental authors as well as modern researchers. Indeed, it has led them to the conclusion that there existed a brotherhood called the *futuwwatiyya*, which is completely contrary to historical reality. I demonstrated in a work that I published some time ago how baseless is the claim that in the fourteenth century the akhīs of Ankara were large landowners who established a kind of republic and that the Ottomans received Ankara from them. This conclusion has now generally been accepted by competent scholars.[50]

Based on a study of the futuwwatnāmes, I also stated in the same work that there existed among the akhīs of Anatolia a tight-knit hierarchy like that of the Freemasons, that special truths were revealed to the devotees according to their rank, and that these features were essentially of *bāṭinī* {esoteric, heretical, Shīʿī} origin.[51] My interpretation in this respect has been supported by Massignon's theory in which he has quite rightly asserted that the question of the origin of the Muslim corporations is related to the Carmathian movement.[52] The fact that, in the Sunnī centers of Anatolia under state control, the akhī organization acquired a Sunnī nature does not prove that this view of their origin is wrong. Among the numerous groups whose origin, character, interaction with other organizations, and general historical evolution I have tried to describe, it is certain that the akhīs in particular played a major role in the founding of the Ottoman state and in the creation of the janissaries. This conclusion, which I was the first to present years ago, has subsequently been confirmed by other scholars using new documents.

Although not directly related to the subject, let me make a brief digression here because of its significance. Franz Taeschner has recently proposed that the futuwwa organization might have had an influence on the Byzantine intellectual Pléthon, who is regarded as one of those who prepared the way for the Renaissance.[53] This idea has not yet been supported by sound evidence, but the question of the kind of influence that futuwwa principles and religious and philosophical currents in the Islamic world in the fourteenth and fifteenth centuries in general had on the new religion that he wanted to establish, which was inspired by Greek mythology and Zoroastrianism, is worthy of serious study. Pléthon spent part of his life at the Ottoman court and in the Turkish milieu. As has been previously described by J. Fallmerayer, he had certain ideas about social reforms which he suggested should be applied to the Peloponnesus.[54] Among his ideas was a very clear desire to imitate, in rather great measure, the structure of contemporary Turkish society.

c. BĀJIYĀN-I RŪM. A third social group mentioned by ʿĀshıq Pasha-Zāde was the *bājiyān-ı rūm*, which was an organization of women. The existence of such a group is not mentioned by any other source. This has rightly seemed to be highly unusual to researchers who, believing this expression to be the result of a copyist's error and also taking into consideration various handwriting features, have asserted that this was either *ḥājiyān-ı rūm*, that is, Anatolian pilgrims, or *bakhshıyān-ı rūm*, being an expression that survived from the Mongol period.[55] Although we know that those who went on the pilgrimage from Anatolia in the fourteenth century were a rather large group, if they had had such a special organization it would have been unique in the Islamic world. Such a possibility is unlikely. As for the word *bakhshı*, it was used in the fourteenth century at the Ilkhānid court to mean, above all, "a secretary who knew the Uighur and Mongol writings." In earlier periods, it meant "saintly person, sorcerer, popular poet." Historically, it cannot even be accepted as a remote possibility that persons with this title formed an important class in Anatolia. Consequently, like it or not, this word must be read as *bājıyān*.

Even if we dismiss all these considerations, the sentence that follows this word in the text shows that it definitely meant an organization of women and, in fact, explains that Ḥājji Bektāsh Velī, the patron saint of the Bektāshīs, was in contact with them. Moreover, clearly related to this is that, in Bektāshī tradition, the title *bajı* was usually given to female members of this religious order. One wonders if this name was that of a ṣūfī group composed of women? To be sure, we know that there were dervish lodges {tekkes} reserved for women in Egypt in Mamlūk times, that women joined shaikhs in Konya in the Seljuk period, and that they were present, albeit veiled, at the meetings of the shaikhs. We have no information, however, on the existence of such a special organization in Anatolia. Bertrandon de la Broquière states that, at the beginning of the fifteenth century, the Dhū ʾl-Qadr beylik had a Turkmen force composed of 30,000 armed men and 100,000 armed women—in another place he says 30,000 instead of 100,000.[56] One wonders if ʿĀshıq Pasha-Zāde uses the expression bājiyān-ı rūm to mean the armed and warlike women of the Turkmen tribes in the march beyliks? For now, this appears to be the best interpretation that comes to mind.[57]

d. ABDĀLĀN-I RŪM. The fourth group mentioned by ʿĀshıq Pasha-Zāde is the *abdālān-ı rūm*, that is, the heterodox dervishes of Anatolia. This group, which is also referred to in some historical sources as the "*erens* of Khurāsān," played an important religio-social role, especially in the fourteenth century. This appears from the fact that all the sources from this century concerning the Ottoman state mention a group of dervishes who had the titles *abdāl* or *bābā* and who, having wooden swords and being in a state of mystical ecstacy, accompanied the first Ottoman sultans in battle. One wonders if the "abdāls of Anatolia" {*Anadolu abdālları*, i.e., abdālān-ı rūm} was the name of a certain order of vagabond dervishes? If not, does this name essentially belong to all the dervishes who were members of the different heterodox orders and were not strangers to each other? In order not to become confused by these questions which have not yet been answered, we need some brief, but clear and concise, information on the religious conditions of Anatolia in the thirteenth and fourteenth centuries and on the nature of the ṣūfī orders that flourished under these conditions. Only then will it be easy to understand the political history of the Anatolian Turks in the late Middle Ages and learn about the religious factors that influenced the founding of the Ottoman state.

With regard to religious policy, the Anatolian Seljuk state remained faithful to the traditions of the Great Seljuk Empire by defending Sunnism and maintaining support for the ʿAbbāsids. The cities under the influence of the state were always strong Sunnī, indeed, Ḥanafī, centers. The madrasas in these cities and the number of religious orders which began to multiply in the thirteenth century generally maintained and strengthened this tendency. This free urban environment, which was conducive to the Neoplatonic theories of the great ṣūfīs like al-Suhrawardī, Ibn al-ʿArabī, Ṣadr al-Dīn al-Qūnawī, and Mawlānā and their pantheistic tendencies, always kept its Sunnī features, although it was far removed from the fanaticism found in contemporary Muslim cities in other parts of the Near East. The claim by the German Orientalist Professor Franz Babinger that "the Seljuks of Anatolia adopted Shīʿism as their official creed {*madhhab*}" is based on no evidence whatsoever.

Around the time of the founding of the Ottoman state, the most prominent religious orders in the cities of Anatolia were the Mawlāwiyya, Rifāʿiyya, and Khalwatiyya. The Jalāliyya, which took its name from Mawlānā Jalāl al-Dīn al-Rūmī and was later more widely known as the Mawlāwiyya, was not established as an order during the lifetime of its namesake. Mawlānā had assembled about him a great many disciples, from the highest aristocracy to the poorest classes of people. In fact, Christians and Jews were included as well. After his death, his successors took advantage of his great fame, opened lodges everywhere and gradually instituted ceremonies and rules for an order. This order, which was based on the high aristocracy and the upper- and middle- class bourgeoisie, was opposed to heterodox groups from its very beginning, as I will describe shortly, and tried to preserve the existing social and political system. Babinger considers this order to be of the same character as Bektāshism, but this allegation is completely counter to reality. Throughout Ottoman history, these two orders flourished as two powerful rivals.

The Rifāʿiyya or Aḥmadiyya order, which had begun to spread in Anatolia in the thirteenth century, was a popular order which, after the Mongol invasion, was influenced by Turco-Mongol shamanism and had its strongest following in Iraq.[58] In the fourteenth century, this order had various lodges in Anatolia. Its devotees were mainly from the poor classes in the cities. It never acquired great importance.

The Khalwatiyya order appeared in Anatolia with the opening of a lodge by Akhī Yūsuf Khalwatī in Niğde at the end of the thirteenth century. Like the Mawlāwiyya and Rifāʿiyya, this was a bourgeois order which maintained its Sunnī form. This order had no significant influence directly on the religious life of the march beyliks. As soon at it took root in Anatolia, however, it established close relations with the akhī organization and thus won over the working class in the cities. In the following centuries, it became rather strong in Arrān, Āzarbāījān, and the Ottoman Empire.

In order to complete this general picture of the urban religious orders in Anatolia at the beginning of the fourteenth century, I will say that one of the oldest Muslim orders, which was associated with the famous Iranian mystic Abū Isḥāq Qāzarūnī and was known variously as the Qāzarūniyya, Isḥāqiyya, or the Murshidiyya, probably also existed around that time in the cities of Anatolia. I have stated in a previous study that this order, which acquired very great importance in the Ottoman Empire in the fifteenth century, had taken root in Anatolia around the end of the fourteenth century.[59] We can infer, however, from an inscription which shows that an Isḥāqī shaikh from Aksaray had a lodge built for this order in Aleppo in 747 (1348 A.D.)[60] that it was probably found in Anatolia at the beginning of the fourteenth century—indeed, perhaps following the Mongol invasion, that is, in the second half of the thirteenth century. We might guess that this missionary order, which had adopted as its most fundamental principle the spreading of religious propaganda and holy war against unbelievers, was probably active in the regions of the beyliks of western Anatolia.

The fact that the Qāzarūniyya obtained a powerful position in the area under Ottoman control around the end of the fourteenth century and was protected by the rulers is evidence for this. This order, which was based on the petty bourgeoisie and working-class, naturally appeared under the guise of Sunnism in roughly the same manner as the other urban orders.

After taking a look at these manifestations of religious life in Anatolia and the ṣūfī movements which took the form of different orders in the great cities, let us turn our attention, with even greater interest, to the villages and nomadic Turkmen tribes, where religious life and ṣūfī movements were more vigorous, exuberant, and sincere and more likely to be transformed into action. Metaphysical ideas and abstract concepts were extremely simplified in this primitive environment and took practical and concrete form. The subtleties of moral philosophy immediately gave way to the harsh rules of life. It is exceedingly important to appreciate this phenomenon in order to understand, above all, the origins of the march beyliks and the Ottoman state among them.

By the beginning of the fourteenth century, dervish propagandists had spread among the small villages and tribes. They had done so to the extent that the village shaikhs became extremely hostile to the ṣūfī poets in the large cities, for example the poet Gülshehrī who was the shaikh of his lodge in Kırshehir and the successor of Akhī Evren, who attracted a large following in the first half of the thirteenth century and was subsequently considered to be the patron saint of the tanners' guild. The Turkmen who settled in the villages or maintained a nomadic life were no doubt firm and very sincere Muslims. Bertrandon de la Broquière, who passed through Anatolia in the first half of the fifteenth century, says that, while going to Bursa from Kütahya followed by a caravan coming from Mecca, some Turks along the road thought he was a pilgrim and kissed his hand and clothing.[61] But the Islam of these Turkmen was not exactly the orthodox Islam of the urban Turks. Instead, it was a *syncrétisme* resulting from a mixture of the old pagan traditions of the early Turks, a simple and popular form of extremist Shīʿism—with a veneer of Ṣūfism—and certain local customs. Because these Turkmen tribes, which were stongly inclined toward "anticipating the mahdī" {i.e., messianism} were the only power that could challenge the central government, there was continuous religio-political propaganda among them. The primary regulators and directors of the spiritual life of the villagers and nomads were the Turkmen shaikhs, called bābās, who were fully reminiscent of the old Turkish shamans. Their strange clothing, uncanonical practices, and exuberant way of life provoked strong criticism from orthodox ṣūfīs. Neither the religious scholars nor the shaikhs who belonged to the bourgeois orders could compete with these bābās in that environment which was completely alien to their mentality. The terrible Bābāʾī insurrection that I mentioned above was prepared and launched by these energetic propagandists. The Bābāʾīs, whom we see for the first time in Anatolia in the thirteenth century, were thrown into battle with their women and children on orders from their shaikhs, whose physical death they believed was impossible. The Bābāʾīs were much more like a sect than a ṣūfī order and resembled the various ʿAlawī parties that we know existed in Anatolia in later centuries.

With respect to religious history, where should one search for the origins of these Turkmen shaikhs and

Bābā'īs? In my view, one must search for their origins partly in the Yasawiyya and partly in the Qalandariyya orders. Established in Central Asia in the twelfth century, the Yasawiyya was the oldest Turkish order. With great speed, it spread to all Turkish countries. This order took root in Anatolia during the great migrations to that region from Transoxiana and Khwārazm that occurred above all after the Mongol invasion. I have previously studied this order in great detail, so I will not say much about it here.[62] I only wish to correct my previously stated interpretation of the orthodox nature of this order, some of the rites of which I showed were related to the old Turkish shamanism. My recent research based on some new documents that I have obtained has convinced me that at the time it was established this order was of a completely heterodox nature. As for the Qalandariyya, which was of the utmost importance for not only the religious history of Anatolia, but also for the history of Ṣūfism in general (even though the simplest monograph has not yet been written on it), let me summarize, unfortunately very briefly, the results of my research on it.

This great order originated from the *Khurāsān school*, or the group which is simply called the Malāmatiyya. After {the death of} Jamāl al-Dīn al-Sāwī (ca. 630 A.H./1232 A.D., {Köprülü gives the erroneous date of 463 A.H./1070–71, cf. *EI*[2], s.v. "Kalandariyya" [Tahsin Yazıcı]}), it flourished in the areas of Syria, Egypt, Iraq, Iran, India, Central Asia, and Anatolia. Because of its strange rites and its devotees' scorn of public opinion, it was strongly attacked by orthodox ṣūfīs. With regard to the clothing of its members, their way of life and even their moral views, this order is somewhat reminiscent of the Indian *sadhus*. Despite certain differences at various times and places, it was bound to the principles of "celibacy, poverty, begging, and courting public reproach by neglecting the outward rites and duties of religion {*melāmet*}." The Qalandars shaved their hair, eyebrows, beards and mustaches and traveled from city to city in rather large groups, carrying their own special banners and beating small drums. Although they had lodges in some cities, they were usually itinerant. It was quite natural that among these groups, which, with few exceptions, were composed of bachelor vagabonds having no understanding of high philosophical concepts or religious experience, the aforesaid principles led to a spiritual nihilism and even to a shocking immorality. It is fairly easy to see how this Qalandriyya order, which also became associated with a poorly understood pantheism and extremist Shīʿī tendencies, later played a disruptive role in the social and moral system.[63]

At the end of the twelfth century, the famous Turkish shaikh Quṭb al-Dīn Ḥaidar founded an order named after him in Khurāsān. Although the bases of this Ḥaidariyya order were taken from the Yasawiyya, it was greatly inspired by the principles of the Qalandariyya. Its members were mostly Turkish youths in Khurāsān.[64]

In the thirteenth century, members of the Qalandariyya and Ḥaidariyya also began to flock into Anatolia like the Yasawī dervishes. The propagandists for these heterodox orders found more fertile ground in the villages and among the nomads than in the cities. Without doubt, the Turkmen bābās who were the instigators of the Bābāʾī uprising were Turkish dervishes who belonged to these extremist ʿAlawī groups, which had largely commingled with each other, and resembled the old Turkish shamans. It is well-known that, after the Mongol invasion, the number of heterodox groups multiplied in the countries of the Muslim Near East, even in the region of the fanatically Sunnī Mamlūk Empire of Egypt and Syria. This development is especially striking in Anatolia when it was under Ilkhānid rule. We know that there were certain Turkmen bābās who had gained important positions in the retinues of the Mongol commanders and at the Ilkhānid court which, during the reign of Öljeitü, had for a while adopted the *ithnā ʿasharī* {Twelver} form of Shīʿism as the state religion. We also know that certain Turkish dervishes went to Anatolia with their disciples under Mongol protection and continued their propaganda there. These Turkmen bābās did not just stay in the villages or among the nomads. They were also found at the Seljuk court and in the company of the march beys. According to Aflākī, the respect that the Seljuk sultan

Rukn al-Dīn Qılıch-Arslan IV showed to a Turkmen shaikh having the byname Bābā Merendī had an extraordinary effect on Mawlānā; and another Turkmen shaikh, who was in the company of the Menteshid ruler Masʿūd Bey, annoyed Mawlānā's grandson, Chelebi ʿĀrif. In any case, around the beginning of the fourteenth century, these Turkmen bābās and Shīʿī propaganda exercised considerable influence in some of the beyliks of western Anatolia. Explicit evidence showing that the Aydınid ruler Khıḍır Bey was a Shīʿī is found in a treaty dated 1348. Furthermore, the first Ottoman rulers had a very protective attitude toward heterodox dervishes.

The new material provided by Qāḍī Aḥmad of Niğde sheds somewhat more light on religious conditions of the time with regard to the aforesaid description. He says that among certain tribes in Anatolia there were those who professed atheism and the principle of *ibāḥiyya* {antinomianism}. He accuses of unbelief and atheism certain nomadic tribes like the Gök Börids and Turgudids, the wood cutters and coal dealers in the province of Luluva (Loulôn), and supporters of an ibāḥī shaikh named Ibrāhīm Ḥājji, who, like a false prophet, attracted, with various tricks and ruses, a large group of ignorant people around Niğde. He also states that there was a group in Anatolia called the Taptukī (or more correctly the Taptuklu), because they were followers of a Turkish shaikh named Taptuk, who offered their daughters, sisters, and wives to guests. This last statement is the oldest existing record of an accusation that the Sunnīs always made against the Kızılbash {semi-political Shīʿī sects in Anatolia}. The other information provided by Qāḍī Aḥmad, although pertaining mainly to the milieu of central Anatolia which he knew of first hand, can also be applied with great confidence to western Anatolia. In any case, this information completely corroborates the conclusions I had reached even before I had obtained it and complements the discussion that I have given above.

These then were the active propagandist and warrior {for the faith} Turkmen bābās who, around the beginning of the fourteenth century, were found among the Turkish villages and Turkmen tribes which had begun to advance once again to the west, toward Byzantine territory. A great many dervishes with the title abdāl—for example Abdāl Mūsā, Abdāl Murad, and Kumral Abdāl, who were in the company of the first Ottoman rulers and who, according to legend, went into battle with wooden swords, captured fortresses, crushed thousands of the enemy with a handful of disciples, and spread Islam—were members of the group which ʿĀshıq Pasha-Zāde called the *rūm abdālları* {abdāls of Anatolia}. As can be seen from my aforesaid discussion, this group can be considered to represent a later form of Bābāʾīsm that came about from a mixture of the traditions of different heterodox groups, like the Yasawiyya, Qalandariyya, and Ḥaidariyya, the traditions of the Turkmen in Anatolia, and local superstitions. It is highly likely that the Torlaks and "dervishes" whom we find in some Eastern and Western works on the Ottoman period are none other than these abdāls. These abdāls, who, in the seventeenth century, were certainly represented by the Bektāshiyya and some other groups in the same catagory, were at first primarily under the influence of the Qalandariyya. But they later recognized Ḥājji Bektāsh Velī as one of their saints and were therefore much more inclined toward Bektāshism after the fifteenth century.

In order to complete this picture of religious life in fourteenth-century Anatolia, and especially of that of the western Anatolian beyliks, let me say a few words about Bektāshism. I have shown in many publications over the years the mistaken conclusions that have been reached on this important subject by Orientalists, although they have devoted more attention to it than to any of the other old Anatolian orders.[65] Some of the objections raised by Professor H. H. Schaeder in this regard[66] and certain misinterpretations resulting from a poor analysis of the contemporary religious life in Anatolia are absolutely refuted by documents that I have recently come across on Bektāshism. Ḥājji Bektāsh, who was the most important successor of the famous Bābāʾī shaikh Bābā Rasūl Allāh (originally called Bābā Isḥāq), gave his name to an order which can generally be considered a continuation of Bābā'ism, the syncretistic nature of which we have seen. The claims that Ḥājji Bektāsh had audiences with the Ottoman rulers and played a role in founding the janissary corps have no historical basis. Although the Bektāshī order was in existence in the fourteenth century, it was not the most important among similar heterodox orders which were extensions of Bābā'ism. It only acquired its importance between the fourteenth {fifteenth in the Fr. ed.} and sixteenth centuries, that is, after absorbing the other heterodox groups. The presence, in the fourteenth century, of the cult of Ḥājji Bektāsh, the Bābā'ī successor, among the abdāls and all other groups which derived from Bābā'ism, led to the belief that all of these groups were Bektāshīs, and thus the importance attributed to Bektāshism in the founding of the Ottoman state was exaggerated. There were, however, followers of Ḥājji Bektāsh in western Anatolia during the founding of the Ottoman state. Let me add that these vagabond groups were the greatest factor in the religious life of the settled and nomadic Turkmen on the frontiers, and also played the most active and decisive role in the conversion of the Christian population. In the Islamization of the Balkans in the fourteenth and fifteenth centuries, the decisive role of the heterodox dervish groups appears to be even clearer and more extensive.

C. The Early History of the Ottoman State

I hope that I have described in general outline the social conditions of both central and western Anatolia before and during the founding of the Ottoman state, the material and spiritual forces encountered there, and the kinds of activities that arose from them. Because Slavic and Byzantine studies, which have made great progress for a century, have rather clearly described the social and political life of the Balkans and Byzantium in the thirteenth and fourteenth centuries, I will not discuss here the external factors which made possible the founding of the Ottoman state, indeed, which facilitated it. Instead, bearing in mind both these external conditions, which are generally well-known, and the social factors of this great historical process, which I have tried to explain to this point, let me first present and describe systematically the stages of the birth and growth of the Ottoman state up to the end of the fourteenth century, and then let me attempt to disentangle the major causative factors, especially the internal factors, of this great event.

1. Historical Events

A small fraction of the Oghuz Qayı Turks who had come to Anatolia and established themselves in various places during the initial Seljuk conquests lived in northwestern Anatolia and on the Turco-Byzantine border around the end of the thirteenth century. One might presume that in the second half of the thirteenth century they were in the company of the powerful Turkish emīr of Paphlagonia, Umur, and fought the Byzantines nearby. The clever and resolute chief of this tribe, Osman, took advantage of the current anarchy in Byzantium and the abandonment of Byzantine lands in Anatolia and slowly began to expand his territory. The first contact between the imperial army and Osman, who threatened the area around Nicaea, occurred when the Byzantines under the command of George Muzalon fought him at Koyunhisarı (Baphaeum) in 1301 (according to Muralt, 1302).[67] Byzantium, which was preoccupied with numerous problems in both Constantinople and the Balkans, and which was struggling against powerful enemies, like the Germiyānids in western Anatolia and the coastal beyliks subject to them, found it impossible to move against Osman for a long time. Certain places, which had to defend themselves with their own forces, were captured. Finally, in 1326, it was the turn of Bursa, which had lost its outlying villages many years previously. Alarmed about the continuous advances of the Ottomans and their threat to Nicaea, the young Byzantine emperor, Andronicus III Palaeologus, attacked the army of Orhan at Pelecanum, present day Maltepe, in 1329 but was defeated; and in 1331 Nicaea passed into the hands of Orhan. In 1337 or 1338, the Ottoman beylik also took possession of Izmit and henceforth controlled the Koja-eli peninsula. From this time to probably 1360, the Ottoman state also succeeded in annexing, piece by piece, the territory of the Karasid beylik. Ibn Baṭṭūṭa and al-ʿUmarī, who discuss the position of the Ottoman state in the last years of the first half of the fourteenth century, mention the actions of Orhan and state that he possessed a powerful army.

After the death of Ghāzī Umur Bey, the powerful ruler of the Aydınid state, Byzantium was occupied with all kinds of internal and extenal problems and even tried very hard to secure the assistance Orhan, who henceforth actively interfered in Byzantine internal affairs. Under these circumstances, the Ottomans, who had begun to establish themselves on the European continent in 1345, seized Gallipoli by taking advantage of a violent earthquake that destroyed the walls of the city's fortress. A great many Turks from Anatolia, and especially Karasi, then went there and settled and Orhan sent certain nomadic tribes there as well. That part of the population of Thrace which was able, fled before the Ottoman invasion and the areas they abandoned were filled with the Turks coming from Anatolia. This movement, which began in 1359, was not a *temporary invasion*, which had up to then been carried out not only by the Ottomans, but also by the other coastal emirates before them, but was a *genuine settlement* of the area. For the first time, the centuries-old Byzantine capital, Constantinople, was able to understand the Ottoman threat in the full sense of the word.

When Murad I ascended the throne, the Turks were firmly settled on the shores of Europe with Gallipoli as their base of forward operations. Indeed, the conquest of Thrace was well advanced. In the campaign of 1360–61, Orhan's experienced commanders had taken possession of the most important strategic places in Thrace.[68] During the sultanate of Murad, which lasted until 1389, the goal of firmly establishing Ottoman rule in the Balkans was reached. Transferring their capital to Edirne, the Ottomans captured the rest of Thrace, Macedonia, and Bulgaria and settled Turkish emigrants in these regions in rather significant numbers. Finally, on the battlefield of Kossovo, they crushed Serbia. The Ottoman state, whose power increased with these victories in the Balkans, also expanded its borders in Anatolia in the reign of Murad. The Ottomans took Ankara and its environs, and an important part of the lands of the Germiyānids and Ḥamīdids, and defeated the Qaramānids. It can definitely be said that, by the time Bayezid I ascended the throne, the Ottoman state, which had become a powerful empire, had been securely established in the Balkans and Anatolia. The fact that this political structure, which Bayezid strengthened and doubled in size, withstood two great tests like the battles of Nicopolis {1396} and Ankara {1402}, one of which ended in a brilliant victory and the other in the capture of the sultan, shows how unshakable were its foundations.

2. *Factors in the Development of the Ottoman State*

After providing this general overview of the century in which the Ottoman state was established, I can briefly list the major causative factors of this great historical enterprise as follows:

a. The presence of the Ottomans on the Turco-Byzantine border, that is, their geographic location. I have shown that a number of other Turkish groups which were on the Byzantine border in western Anatolia also established political entities, some even preceded the Ottomans and were more powerful, and I explained all the reasons for this.

b. The Turkish beyliks on the Ottoman borders took no hostile action against this new entity. Osman, who at first may have been subject to Umur, the emīr of Paphlagonia, carried out independent operations from the time of Umur's death until Paphlagonia passed into the hands of the Jāndārids, and probably certain minor powers in that area joined him during this confused period. Because the Jāndārids were occupied on the one hand with taking possession of the coastal regions along the Black

Sea, in order to prevent possible naval raids, and, on the other, with maintaining their position against the Ilkhānid governors in central Anatolia, and then against Eretna and the other Turkish principalities with which they had a common border, they could not look unfavorably on this small entity that was struggling against the Byzantines.

As for the Germiyānids, this powerful dynasty, which was in a position to resist successfully the major political powers in central and southern Anatolia, was also busy conquering Byzantine territory. After the rise in power of coastal beyliks like those of the Aydınids and Ṣārūkhānids, which at first were subject to the Germiyānids, and in fact had originally been established by their military commanders, their state became an inland state. Once the Germiyānids captured Karahisar and the lands subject to the Inānjids, they were only concerned about maintaining their position against the Ḥamīdids, and especially the Qaramānids.

With regard to the Menteshids, Aydınids, Ṣārūkhānids, and Karasids, the routes of conquest that they followed and their objectives never conflicted, at least initially, with those of the Ottomans. For a while, the Byzantines incited them against the Ottomans, but this proved to be fruitless because they had other enemies to face. Thus, the general political situation in Anatolia left the field clear to the Ottomans when they began their operations.

c. The conditions which facilitated the entry of the Ottomans into Europe after they took the borderlands which they had shared with Byzantium in Asia, and which facilitated their firm establishment in the Balkans, have been rather clearly explained by many scholars, above all specialists in Slavic and Byzantine studies, who have worked on the medieval history of southeastern Europe. I will therefore pass over in silence these aspects of our subject which are basically well-known to the scholarly world.

d. The first Ottoman rulers, like those of the other beyliks on the western frontier, found among the Turkish elements—nomads, villagers, and city dwellers—who had come to the western border in the second half of the thirteenth century, sufficient material and moral forces to allow them to capture Byzantine territory in Anatolia and become firmly established on it. While the coastal beyliks suffered from continuous and always unproductive wars against not only the Byzantines but also the Latin naval forces, the Ottoman beylik slowly but surely, step by step, expanded its borders without exhausting itself and continuously increased its strength. Before the Ottomans captured Gallipoli, the Christian world did not even care that they existed, while the brilliant but fruitless {naval} campaigns of Ghāzī Umur Bey had outraged the Mediterranean Christian world, led by the pope, and made it necessary {for the Christians} to seize Izmir on his death. It is necessary to take into account this special geographic location which distinguished the Ottomans from the other frontier beyliks at the time of the founding of their state, namely, the fact that the only adversary they faced was Byzantium. If not, the other factors affecting the rise of the Ottoman State would apply almost equally well to the founding of the other coastal beyliks.

e. In all the maritime beyliks except that of the Ottomans, the state was considered to be the common property of the entire {ruling} family. Each prince independently ruled the area that belonged to him. In theory, the oldest member of the family had a kind of right of sovereignty over the others, but he could only enforce it when he had the physical power to do so. When Mehmed Bey became the Aydınid ruler in Birgi, his youngest son was at his side while his other sons were made rulers of other areas {of the state}. Each one had his own separate force. Umur Bey embarked upon his first Gallipoli campaign against the wishes of his father. Although Umur had an older brother, he ascended the throne of the beylik after the death of his father upon the insistence of his paternal uncles and his brother Khıḍır Bey. Such conditions frequently caused internal rivalries and struggles in all the coastal beyliks and weakened them. In the Ottoman state, however, all power was in the hands of a single ruler. Thus, it appears that Murad I, as his son Bayezid was later to do, did away with his brothers in order not to have any rivals or claimants to the throne. The principle of *indivisibility of sovereignty* was a major factor in preventing the Ottoman state from encountering any significant domestic instability in the fourteenth century.[69] One wonders if this was the consequence of a juridical development or an application of the personal experience of the rulers? For now, nothing can be said about this. Just let me state that this was in accordance with the principles of Islamic public {*amme*} law.

f. The rapidity with which the Ottomans entered Europe and became firmly established in Gallipoli, after easily taking an important part of Karasid territory, was a major factor in strengthening the structure of their state, because a great many nomadic elements, poor villagers and sipāhīs, who wanted to acquire rich timars in Rumelia, went from central Anatolia and such coastal beyliks as those of the Karasids, Ṣārūkhānids, Aydınids, and Menteshids to Thrace and Macedonia in order to find and settle rich empty lands. In addition to the masses that the state transferred there in order to populate the region, those who went of their own choice were probably also in large numbers. A great many of the people from the coastal beyliks had long known of this rich and beautiful region called Rumelia, for they had gone there under the command of their beys. By attracting them to this region, the Ottoman state continuously increased its power at the expense of its neighbors in Anatolia. The transfer of such large groups of Turks from Anatolia to Rumelia also continued in the fifteenth century.

g. The Ottomans easily carried out their conquests in the Balkans without suffering any significant loss of men. During these conquests, considerable booty and many prisoners were taken from the captured areas. One fifth of these prisoners, most of whom were young children, were reserved for the state and were sent to Anatolia where they were educated among the Turks. After learning Turkish and becoming Muslims, they were employed in military service.

The military commanders who owned large timars in Anatolia, as well as the holders of smaller timars, either sold their share of the prisoners or, according to Islamic custom, trained and used them in their own service. We know that in the first half of the fifteenth century, there existed villages in Anatolia which were set aside as endowments {waqfs}, along with their Christian population, for certain purposes. Although we cannot say for sure, we might guess that these villages were composed of such prisoners. If this were the case, it would show that only some of these prisoners—perhaps the young ones—were converted to Islam while the majority were employed in agriculture by the great landowners on their own lands.

The people in places that were captured by peaceful means were left where they were upon payment of certain taxes. The vagabond dervish groups which I described above were busy continuously spreading Islamic propaganda among the Christian population. One could imagine that Islam spread easily among heretical groups, like the Bogomils who were hostile to the Orthodox Church. Conversions also took place, of course, among the aristocracy for economic and psychological reasons. But it could be said that such conversions did not take place on a very large scale in the fourteenth century. We only see them later, especially in Bosnia and Albania, in the fifteenth and even the sixteenth centuries.[70] The state did not interfere in any of this, nor did it apply any pressure to convert. It always respected religious freedom, the privileges of the clerical classes, and the customs and traditions of the various communities.

h. The janissary force that was composed of the aforesaid young prisoners was at first a standing infantry in the company of the ruler. The cavalry force created by the timar-holding sipāhīs, however, constituted the greatest military force of the state. In the fourteenth century, the janissaries were not of major importance. It was only in the fifteenth century during the reign of Murad II that the principle of devshirme was instituted in a systematic manner.

i. The Ottoman state maintained the principle, which had been followed by the Seljuks, of dividing captured lands into timars of different values and granting them to sipāhīs in return for military service. The largest grants, *zeāmets* {very large timars} and khāṣṣ, were given to the most important commanders on condition that they provide soldiers in proportion to the income from these lands. The passing of the position of sipāhī from father to son created a landed aristocracy with very firm roots in the country. This class, whose interests and income were based on the economic development of the areas that had been assigned to them, that is, on the prosperity of the villager class, acted to some degree as representatives of the government on their own large estates. They played a major role in both the political development and economic prosperity of the Ottoman state in the fifteenth century. Let me repeat, as I have shown elsewhere at great length, that this system was not taken from Byzantium but was a continuation of a practice found in the Great Seljuk Empire.[71]

j. The civil, military, and judicial organization of the Ottoman state was essentially a continuation of that of the Anatolian Seljuks, but it was also partly under the influence of the Ilkhānid organization and somewhat less under that of the Mamlūks of Egypt. I have previously discussed this subject rather extensively and will not attempt to do so again here. With very few exceptions, the Ottoman state found the elements that it needed for every aspect of its organization in the fourteenth century among the Turks. The great men of state and military commanders—with one or two exceptions like the Mihal Oghulları—were all members of the Turkish aristocracy. This aristocracy, which arose concurrently with the Ottoman dynasty and founded the Ottoman state with it, kept the entire government in their own hands in the fourteenth century. They produced the great commanders, skillful administrators, talented organizers and shrewd diplomats.

k. In addition to all these factors, one must also take into consideration the organizational skills of the first Ottoman rulers: Osman, Orhan, and Murad, especially the latter. A *déterminisme* which, mistakenly, does not take into account the dominant role of great and creative individuals in social life disregards a very important factor in that social life and historical development.

In light of all these facts, we can say the following about the reality of the origins of the Ottoman state from the point of view of the historical march of the Turks of Anatolia: this state was not a new organism, a new ethnic and political entity having no relationship to the extinct Seljuk sultanate or the Anatolian beyliks which succeeded it. On the contrary, as I have explained above, it was a new *synthesis*, a new historical composite which arose from the political and social evolution of the Anatolian Turks in the thirteenth and fourteenth centuries, the same Turks who had previously created the states of the Anatolian Seljuks and Dānishmendids and the Anatolian beyliks.

NOTES

Introduction

1. I first broadly explained this new approach, with special respect to literary history, in my article "Türk edebiyat tarihinde usul" {all Turkish titles mentioned in the notes are translated in the bibliography}, *Bilgi Mecmuası*, 1 (1329/1913), 3–52. Until the appearance of this article, it had never been considered by Western or Eastern researchers, and was even rather strange and startling to scholars bound to the old traditions. Because literary history was a "branch of history," I showed that this approach should apply to all branches of Turkish history. Let me add to this the following two studies which were made in complete conformity with this point of view: "Türk edebiyatında āşık tarzı'nın menşe ve tekāmülü hakkında bir tecrübe," *MTM*, (1331), nr. 1, 5–46, and "Selçukīler zamanında Anadoluda Türk medeniyeti," *MTM*, (1331), nr. 5, 193–232.

2. "Because the very limited and general works and monographs written up to now on our literary history in the East and West are for the most part without scientific value, the problem of the general evolution of Turkish literature is still an unsolved mystery for the scholarly world. Unfortunately no one, from Hammer to Gibb and from the old writers of official memoranda to some of the rare researchers of today, has essentially been able to understand that it is necessary to study and analyze the literary development of the entire Turkish nation, from inner Asia to the shores of the Mediterranean, at least in the thirteenth and fourteenth centuries, 'as a *whole*.' In the hands of scholars who consider the different branches of the Turks to be separate nations which had no contact with each other, and who do not understand the ties and relationships among them, and who see no need to

study the general history of the Turks as a whole, this important part of world history would remain a mystery forever. Fortunately, the historical research which has modestly begun in our country in the past six or seven years has shown the error of this point of view which Orientalists have pursued up to now. It is obvious what route must be followed in order to study our past and bring it to life. The future will show what important results this new approach will have in the study of all branches of Turkish history," *Türk edebiyatında ilk mutasavvıflar* (Istanbul, 1918), p. 6.

3. {İbrahim and Cevriye Artuk indicate that the Qayı seal (*damga*) first appears on the coinage of Murad II, *İstanbul arkeoloji müzeleri teşhirdeki islami sikkeler kataloğu* (Istanbul, 1970–74), II, 467. Philip Remler mentions no seal on the coinage of Orhan in his "Ottoman, Isfendiyarid, and Eretnid Coinage: A Currency Community in Fourteenth-Century Anatolia," *American Numismatic Society Museum Notes*, 25 (1980), 167–88.}

Chapter 1

1. {Reviews of Gibbons' book in} *JA*, 11th series, 9 (1917), 345–50; *Journal des Savants*, (April 1917), 157–66.

2. "Das Problem der Entstehung des osmanischen Reiches," *Zeitschrift für Semitistik und verwandte Gebiet*, 2 (1924), 246–71.

3. *Von alten osmanischen Reich* (Tübingen, 1930).

4. "The Rise of the Ottoman Turks and its Historical Background," *American Historical Review*, 37 (1931–32), 488–505.

5. *EI*[1], s.v. "Türks," pt. IV, "History."

6. {Gibbons' *Foundation of the Ottoman Empire*, though reprinted (London, 1968), is now largely ignored. Wittek's theory as presented in "Deux chapitres de l'histoire des Turcs de Roum," *Byzantion*, 11 (1936), 285–319, became the explanation of choice after Gibbons. This came about to a considerable extent because most students of the subject simply accepted what Wittek had presented and rejected, in his *Rise of the Ottoman Empire*, as the main argument of Köprülü's *Les Origines* without reading it.}

7. {"Auszüge aus Neśrī's Geschichte des osmānischen Hauses,"} *ZDMG*, 13 {(1859), 176–218}.

8. E. Lavisse and A. Rambaud, *Histoire générale {de IVe siècle à nos jour* (Paris, 1893–1901)}, III, 822–24.

9. "Der Islam in Kleinasien. {Neue Wege der Islamforschung}," *ZDMG*, N.F., 76 (1922), 132.

10. *Histoire de l'Asie* (Paris, 1921–22), I, 274.

11. *Ṭabaqāt-i nāṣirī* (Persian text) (Calcutta, 1864), p. 9.

12. In the still unpublished part of Rashīd al-Dīn where he discusses the traditions of the Oghuz Turks (numerous manuscripts in Istanbul and Paris). {Later published by Zeki Validi Togan, *Oğuz destani* (Istanbul, 1972), p. 73.}

13. Manuscripts in the Bibliothèque Nationale, supplement to the Persian manuscripts, nr. 1559. {This *saljūqnāme* has been published in facsimile and translated by Feridun Uzluk as *Tarih-i āl-i Selçuk (Selçuknāme) der Anadolu: Anadolu Selçukluları devleti tarihi* (Ankara, 1952). See p. 6 of the Persian text.}

14. {V. L. Ménage used the "dream of Ertughrul" in masterly fashion to develop the order of composition of some early Ottoman chronicles. See his "On the Recensions of Uruj's 'History of the Ottomans,'" *BSOAS*, 30 (1967), 314–22.}

15. Bāqī, *Faḍā'il al-jihād*, Turkish manuscript from the sixteenth century, numerous copies of which are found in various libraries.

16. Cf. the Persian text, p. 95. {Now edited and translated by Irene Mélikoff as *La geste de Melik Danişmend* (Paris, 1960).}

17. For this famous romance, see my *Türk edebiyatı tarihi* (Istanbul, 1926), pp. 304–06.

18. Cf. the Persian text, (Bibliotheca Indica: Calcutta, 1887), II, 239.

19. *Seyāḥatnāme* {Istanbul, 1896–1938}, VIII, 209. For a another varient, see J. G. Frazer, *Le rameau d'or* (Paris, 1924), p. 267, {in the original English, *The Golden Bough* (New York, 1942). With respect to folklore, see the interesting compendium of Hasan Özdemir, *Die altosmanischen Chroniken als Quelle zur türkischen Volkskunde* (Freiburg, 1975)}.

20. {Köprülü begins to lay the groundwork here for his theory, which later scholars have not accepted (nor discussed), that

the ancestors of the Ottomans arrived before the thirteenth century. See Claude Cahen, "La première pénétration turque en Asie-Mineure," reprinted in *Turcobyzantina et Oriens Christianus* London, 1974), article I, 5–67.}

21. Let me give just one example, Ch. Diehl, *Byzance: grandeur et décadence* (Paris, 1919), pp. 325–26.

22. {Köprülü's assertion here is too strong. It must be remembered that he wrote at a time of great nationalist feeling in Turkey, when the Turkish Republic was seeking its identity and Atatürk was at the height of his power. Contrary to Köprülü's claim, see the examples related by Palamas, ed. Anna Phillipides-Braat, "La captivité de Palamas chez les Turcs: dossier et commentaire," *Travaux et Mémoirs, Centre de Recherche d'Histoire et Civilization Byzantines*, 7 (1979), 109–22, and in Jean Darrouzès, *Les régestes de 1310 à 1376*, fasc. 5, vol. 1 of *Les régestes des actes du patriarcat de Constantinople* (Paris, 1977), vis. Orhan's judge.}

23. {Giese, "Das Problem der Entstehung des osmanischen Reiches," *Zeitschrift für Semitistik und verwandte Gebiet*. Köprülü's quotation is not in this article, but is a rough summary of part of it.}

24. "Anadolu'da islāmiyet," *Darülfünün Edebiyat Fakültesi Mecmuası*, 2 (1922), offprint pp. 84, 88.

25. "Osmanlı imparatorluğunun kuruluşu meselesi," *Hayat Mecmuası*, nrs. 11 and 12 (1927).

26. {Article title unidentified.} *Zapiski Vostochnago Otdyeleniya Imperatorskago Russkago Arkheologicheskago Obshchestva*, vol. 18, pp. 124f.

27. {Al-Aqsarāyī's *Musāmarat* has been edited by Osman Turan (Ankara, 1944). It has been translated into Turkish by M. Nuri Gençosman as *Selçuklu devletleri tarihi* (Ankara, 1943), and a summary German translation of the fourth and last part has been made by Fikret Işıltan as *Die Seltschuken Geschichte des Akserayī* (Leipzig, 1943).}

28. {On Qāḍī Aḥmad, see Yaşar Yücel, *Kadı Burhaneddin Ahmed ve devleti (1344–1398)* (Ankara, 1970).}

29. {On Astarābādī, see Heinz Giesecke, *Das Werk des ʿAzīz ibn Ardaşīr Astarābādī, eine Quelle zur Geschichte des Spätmittelalters in Kleinasien* (Leipzig, 1940).}

30. {"Over de Geschiedenis der Seldjuken van Klein-Azie,"} *Verslagen en Mededeelingen d. k. Akad. v. Wetensch. Afd. letterkunde*, 3rd series, part 9, {Amsterdam}, (1893), {133–53}. {On the *saljq̄nāme*, see nt. 13 above.}

31. P. Wittek, *Das Fürstentum Mentesche* (Istanbul, 1934), p. 50, n. 2. {On Shikārī, see Köprülü's "Anadolu Selçukluları tarihinin yerli kaynakları," *Belleten*, 7 (1943), p. 400, nt. 1, Leiser's translation, nt. 34, and cf. Rudi Lindner, *Nomads and Ottomans in Medieval Anatolia* (Bloomington, Indiana, 1983), pp. 145–47.}

32. {Yınanç published the text in 1928 and an introduction in 1930, both in Istanbul. See also the partial publication by Irene Mélikoff, *Le destan d'Umur Pacha* (Paris, 1954), and the evaluation in Paul Lemerle, *L'emirat d'Aydın, Byzance et l'Occident* (Paris, 1957).}

33. {For a catagorization of these sources, see Köprülü's "Anadolu Selçukluları tarihinin yerli kaynakları."}

34. "De la valeur historique des mémoirs des derviches tourneurs," *JA*, 11th series, 19 (1922), 308–17.

35. Cf. "Anadolu beylikleri tarihine ait notlar," *TM*, 2 (1928), 1–32.

36. {On epigraphy, see Ét. Combe et al., *Répertoire chronologique d'épigraphie arabe* (Cairo, 1931–64), index (Cairo, 1975). On numismatics, see Artuk, *İstanbul arkeoloji müzeleri . . . kataloğu*, and Gilles Hennequin, *Catalogue des monnaies musulmanes de la Bibliothèque Nationale*, vol. 5, *Asie pré-mongole: les Salğuqs et leur successeurs* (Paris, 1985).}

37. F. Babinger, *Die Geschichtsschreiber der Osmanen und ihre Werke* (Leipzig, 1927). {Ahmedi is now available in two different editions (Istanbul, 1947 and 1988); Rūhī is in fact a reworked Uruj Bey; Kemal Pasha-Zāde's sections on Osman, Orhan, Mehmed II and Selim I have been published (see the bibliography in EI^2, s.v. "Kemāl Pas̲ha-Zāde" [V. L. Ménage]); and Konevī has been published in Turkish translation (Istanbul, 1947). On the relationships among these texts, see Ménage, "The Beginnings of Ottoman Historiography," in Bernard Lewis and Peter Holt, eds., *Historians of the Middle East* (Oxford, 1962), pp. 168–179.}

38. Mükrimin Halil {Yınanç}, *Düstūrnāme-i Enverī* {Istanbul, 1928–30}, introduction, I, 61.

39. *MTM*, nrs. 1 and 2, {1331}; {Mehmed ʿArif ed.} in *TOEM*, {supplements to years 3 and 4 (1328 and 1329)}; {Fr. Kraelitz, "Ḳānūnnāme Sultan Meḥmeds des Eroberers,"} *MOG*, 1 {1921–22}. {Now see especially Ö. L. Barkan, *XV. ve XVI. asırlarda osmanlı imparatorluğunda ziraī ekonominin hukukī ve malī esasları* (Istanbul, 1943). Additional *kānūnnāmes* have been published by R. Anhegger and H. İnalcık (Ankara, 1956), N. Beldiceanu (Paris, 1960), U. Heyd (Oxford, 1973), and others. See *EI*[2], s.v. "Ḳānūn," (Halil İnalcık).}

40. Most of these old official documents were published in *TOEM*.

41. {There are more than a few differences. Cf. Ménage, "The *Menāqib* of Yakhshi Faqīh," *BSOAS*, 26 (1963), 50–54.}

42. *TOEM*, nrs. 77–81.

43. {Köprülü did not know Greek and therefore discounted Byzantine sources. See, e.g., the new edition and translation of Pachymeres by Vitalien Laurent and Albert Failler, *Relations historiques / Georges Pachymeres* (Paris, 1984); the new German translation of Gregoras by Jan Louis van Dieten, *Rhomaische Geschichte = Historia Rhomaike [von] Nikephoros Gregoras* (Stuttgart, 1973–88), and Cantacuzenus by Georgios Fatouros and Tilman Krischer, *Geschichte / Johannes Kantakuzenus* (Stuttgart, 1982–86); Peter Schreiner, ed. and trans., *Die byzantinischen Kleinchroniken* (Vienna, 1975–79); and the collected papers of Elizavet Zachariadou, *Romania and the Turks* (London, 1985).}

44. "Bizans müesseselerinin osmanlı müesseselerine te'siri hakkında bāzı mülāhazalar," {an English translation by Gary Leiser is forthcoming}, *THİTM*, 1 (1931), 165–313.

45. {Köprülü was right in maintaining that a strict chronological treatment of the material on early Ottoman history is impossible, but the veracity of more early events than he expected has been confirmed. See, e.g., Irène Beldiceanu-Steinherr, "La conquête d'Andrinople par les Turcs: la pénétration turque en Thrace et la valeur des chroniques ottomanes," *Traveaux et Mémoires*, 1 (1965), 439–61.}

Chapter 2

1. {Anthony Bryer has demonstrated the importance of Trebizond in the thirteenth and fourteenth centuries. See his *Em-*

pire of Trebizond and the Pontos (London, 1980) and Bryer and David Winfield, *The Byzantine Monuments and Topography of the Pontos* (Washington, D.C., 1985).}

2. A. A. Vasiliev, *Histoire de l'Empire Byzantin* (Paris, 1932), II, 186.

3. *Histoire de la vie byzantine. {Empire et civilization}* (Bucharest, 1934), III, 103.

4. Iorga mistakenly gives the name ʿIzz al-Dīn Kai-Kāʾūs to the sultan who was killed in the battle.

5. {Alexios G. C. Savvides, *Byzantium in the Near East* (Thessalonike, 1981), sheds new light on Byzantine-Turkish relations in the generation after 1204.}

6. {On the Bābāʾī revolt, now see Ahmet Yaşar Ocak, *La revolte de Baba Resul* (Ankara, 1989), who uses sources unknown to Köprülü.}

7. {This account of the fate of the followers of Sarı Saltuk must be revised in light of Wittek, "Yazijioghlu ʿAli on the Christian Turks of the Dobruja," *BSOAS*, 14 (1952), 639–68.}

8. According to the new information provided in the *Saljūqnāme* (Bibliothèque Nationale, Persian supplement, nr. 1553). See also İsmail Hakkı {Uzunçarşılı}, *Kütahya Şehri* (Istanbul, 1932).

9. {On the *beyliks*, see Uzunçarşılı's general survey *Anadolu beylikleri* (Ankara, 1937), and more recently Claude Cahen's *Pre-Ottoman Turkey* (New York, 1968) and *La Turquie pré-ottomane* (Istanbul, 1988), which only partially supersedes the former work, and Osman Turan's *Selçuklular zamanında Türkiye tarihi* (Istanbul, 1971). Among the more specific studies are Barbara Flemming, *Landschaaftsgeschichte von Pamphylien, Pisidien und Lykien im Spätmittelalter* (Wiesbaden, 1964); Himmet Akın, *Aydın oğulları tarihi hakkında bir araştırma*, 2nd ed. (Ankara, 1968); Mustafa Çetin Varlık, *Germiyan-oğulları tarihi, 1300–1429* (Ankara, 1974); and Yaşar Yücel, *Çoban-oğulları, Candar-oğulları beylikleri* (Ankara, 1980).}

10. {Köprülü's implication that the "earlier people of Anatolia" were not fully Hellenized cannot be maintained unless he believed that the Armenian and Syrian Christians were in especially large numbers. See, e.g., Speros Vryonis, *The Decline of Medieval Hellenism in Asia Minor* (Berkeley, California, 1971).}

11. S. Guyard, *Géographie d'Aboulféda* (Paris, 1883), II, pt. 2, p. 134. {Abū ʾl-Fidā's figure of 200,000 is, of course, an exaggeration. See Cahen, "Ibn Saʿīd sur l'Asie Mineure seldjuqide," in *Turcobyzantina*, article XI, 41–50.}

12. One encounters certain evidence to support the ideas that I have advanced in the various sources for the period in question.

13. According to sources like Rashīd al-Dīn's *Jāmiʿ al-tawārīkh*, Müneccim-başı's *Jāmiʿ al-duwal*, and Shikārī's *Vekāyiʿ-nāmeleri*. {On the latter, see above, ch. 1, nt. 31.}

14. Astarābādī, *Bazm u razm* (Istanbul, 1928).

15. I will publish a study on the new ethnic elements that appeared in Anatolia after the Mongol invasion. {Cf. his "Osmanlı imparatorluğunun etnik menşei meseleler," *Belleten*, 7 (1943), 219–313; and idem, "Kay kabilesi hakkında yeni notlar," *Belleten*, 8 (1944), 421–52.}

16. L. de Mas Latrie, *L'île de Chypre*, *{sa situation présente et ses souvenirs du moyen-âge}* (Paris, 1879), p. 246.

17. {Most of the "Mongols" were in fact Turks. See John Masson Smith, Jr., "Mongol manpower and Persian population," *JESHO*, 18 (1975), 271–99.}

18. G. Pauthier, *Le livre de Marco Polo* (Paris, 1865), I, 35–37; A. Charignon, *Le livre de Marco Polo* (Pekin, 1924), I, 34. {For an English translation, Henry Yule and Henri Cordier, *The Book of Ser Marco Polo*, 3rd ed. (London, 1921). Whether or not there was a Turkish majority in the thirteenth century is a matter of great dispute. Köprülü ignored the evidence of William of Rubruck, among others.}

19. Bertrandon de la Broquière, *Le voyage d'outremer*, ed. Ch. Schefer (Paris, 1892), pp. 82–98.

20. {There was no connection between the Paulicians and this movement. See Nina Garsoian, *The Paulician Heresy* (The Hague, 1967).}

21. "Les origines du Bektachisme," *Actes du Congrès International d'Histoire des Religions {tenu à Paris en 1923}* (Paris, 1926), II, 404–05.

22. {For recent research on the society of Anatolia from the

ninth to the thirteenth centuries, see Michael Hendy's *Studies in the Byzantine Monetary Economy* (Cambridge, 1985), and *The Economy, Fiscal Administration and Coinage of Byzantium* (Northampton, 1989). Köprülü paints too bleak a picture of the Anatolian countryside.}

23. {See Faruk Sümer, "Anadolu'ya yalnız göçebe Türkler mi geldi?" *Belleten*, 24 (1960), 567–94.}

24. All of these questions will be critically studied in the book that I am preparing on the economic history of medieval Turkey {never published}. {Now see the works of Irène Beldiceanu-Steinherr on the Seljuk land regime as reflected in Ottoman documents, e.g., "Fiscalité et formes de possession de la terre arable dans l'Anatolie pré-ottomane," *JESHO*, 19 (1976), 233–322.}

25. W. Heyd, *Histoire du commerce du Levant au moyen-âge* {Paris, 1923}, I, 301–04.

26. L. de Mas Latrie, *L'île de Chypre*, pp. 209–10.

27. G. I. Bratianu, *Recherches sur le commerce génois dans la Mer Noire au XIIIe siècle* (Paris, 1929), p. 165.

28. L. de Backer, *Guillaume de Rubrouck* (Paris, 1877), pp. 292–93. {English translation by Christopher Dawson as *The Mongol Mission: Narratives and Letters of the Franciscan Missionaries in Mongolia and China in the Thirteenth and Fourteenth Centuries* (New York, 1955).}

29. {Zeki Validi Togan, "Moğollar devrinde Anadolu'nun iktisadī vaziyeti,"} *THİTM*, 1 (1931), 1–42 {an English translation by Gary Leiser is forthcoming in *Annales Islamologiques*}.

30. *Recueil des historiens des Croisades: Documents arméniens* {Paris, 1869–1906}, II, 271–72; H. Omont, "Notice du MS. Nov. Acq. Franç. 10.050 de la Bibliothèque Nationale contenant un nouveau texte français {de 'La fleur des histoires de la terre d'orient'} de Haython," *Notices et Extraits {des Manuscrits de la Bibliothèque Nationale et Autres Bibliothèques}*, 38 (1903), 262–63.

31. *Les villes du moyen-âge* (Brussels, 1927), p. 55. {English translation, *Medieval Cities* (Princeton, New Jersey, 1925). There is a dispute of long-standing about the nature of the "Islamic city," see, e.g., A. H. Hourani and S. M. Stern, eds. *The Islamic City* (Oxford, 1970).}

32. This event is very significant. It is recorded in biographical sources like those of Aflākī and Sipahsālār and was corroborated and used in the poetry of Mawlānā's son Sultan Veled in particular.

33. See the studies in F. W. Hasluck's *Christanity and Islam under the Sultans* (Oxford, 1929).

34. Iorga, *Histoire de la vie byzantine*, III, 18, 227. There is additional evidence in the Islamic sources to support this assertion.

35. {This statement is a bit extreme. Cf., e.g., Vryonis, *The Decline of Medieval Hellenism in Asia Minor*, pp. 351–402.}

36. {Faruk Sümer has described one of these fairs, *Yaban Pazarı: An Important International Fair in the Saljuq Period* (Istanbul, 1985).}

37. H. Corbin, "Pour l'anthropologie philosophique: {un traité persan inédit de Suhrawardī d'Alep}," *Recherches Philosophiques*, 2 (1932–33), 376.

38. M. Fuad Köprülüzāde {i.e., Köprülü}, *Türk edebiyatı tarihi*, I, 243–52, 281–322; idem, *Türk edebiyatında ilk mutasavvıflar*, pp. 213–86. The following writers have made a detailed analysis of the latter work: L. Bouvat, {"Les premiers mystiques dans la littérature turque,"} *Revue de Monde Musulman*, 43 (1921), 236–82; Huart, {"Les anciens derviches turcs,"} *Journal des Savants*, 20 (1922), 5–18; and Th. Menzel, {"Köprülüzāde Mehmed Fuād's Werk über die ersten Mystiker in der türkischen Literatur,"} *KCA*, 2 {1926–32}, 281–310, 345–57, 406–22.

Chapter 3

1. Grousset, *Histoire de l'Asie*, I, 273–74, "The founders of the Ottoman state were Oghuz Turks or Qanghlıs who originated from the Aral-Caspian area," and III, 423, "Thus at that time a minor chief from the Qanghlı tribe. . ."

2. Abdülkadir, " 'Orun' ve 'ülüş' meselesi," *THİTM*, 1 (1931), 121–33.

3. J. H. Kramers, "Wer war Osman?" *Acta Orientalia*, 6 {1928}, 242.

4. Abulgāzī Bahādur Khān, *Shajara-i terākima* (the genealogies of the Turkmen). On the importance of this work, see *EI*[1], s. v. "Turkmens," my article on Turkmen literature.

5. Repeated this time by Diehl, *La société byzantine à l'époque des Comnènes* (Paris, 1929), p. 41.

6. {Although Köprülü tries to make the point that Osman's tribe was related to the Qayı, he perhaps places too much weight on the power of nomad opinion. Moreover, he regards a tribe as a strictly consanguinous organization. Wittek had demolished the Qayı genealogies in his "Der Stammbaum der Osmanen," *Der Islam*, 14 (1925), 94–100, and again in his *Rise of the Ottoman Empire*. In the latter, he made the Qayı genealogy the central point of Köprülü's present work, which it clearly is not. For Köprülü's criticism of Wittek, see his "Osmanlı imparatorluğunun etnik menşei meseleleri."}

7. W. Bang and J. Marquart, *Osttürkische Dialektstudien* (Berlin, 1914), pp. 187–94.

8. P. Pelliot, "À propos des Comans," *JA*, 11th series, 15 (1920), 136.

9. Németh's article {a review of A. Fischer, *Die Vokalharmonie der Endungen an den Fremdwörtern des Türkischen*} in *ZDMG*, 75 (1921), 278; Brockelmann, "Alttürkestanische Volkspoesie I," *Asia Major*, 1 (1923), offprint, p. 14; idem, *Das Nationalgefühl der Türken im Licht der Geschichte* (Halle, 1918), p. 17.

10. *Türk edebiyatında ilk mutasavvıflar*, pp. 145–46.

11. "Oğuz etnolojisine dair tarihi notlar," *TM*, 1 (1925), 187–91.

12. See *EI*[1], s.v. "Ḳāyī" {Barthold} and "Türks" {pt. IV, "History," (Kramers)}. {Köprülü seems determined to show that the Ottomans had no relationship to the Mongols, as his previous assertion that the Ottomans arrived in Anatolia before the thirteenth century clearly implies. Most scholars today believe that they, in fact, did arrive in the thirteenth century.}

13. {These place names do not prove a particular arrival date of the Ottomans or anyone else.}

14. *Histoire des Mongols de la Perse* {an ed. and trans. of part of Rashīd al-Dīn} (Paris, 1836), pp. 242–43.

15. *Recueil des historiens des Croisades: Historiens orientaux* {Paris, 1872–1906}, II, pt. 1, p. 23, IV, 438, 452, 454, 457, 469.

16. *Géographie d'Abulféda*, II, pt. 2, p. 134.

17. Ed., *Recueil de textes et de traductions* (Paris, 1889), I, 43.

18. Kamāl al-Dīn {Ibn al-ᶜAdīm}, *Histoire d'Alep* {a trans. of *Zubdat al-ḥalab fī ta'rīkh Ḥalab*} (Paris, 1900), p. 107. Blochet regarded the word uc to be the same as the word Oghuz, "Le pays de Tchata et les Ephtalites," *Atti della Reale Accademia dei Lincei. Rendiconti*, 6th series, 1 (1925), 335–36. There is no historical basis on which to establish this identity whatsoever.

19. See {Ḥamd Allāh Mustawfī Qazvīnī's} *Ta'rīkh-i Guzīda* {London, 1910–13}; also {Huart's trans. of Aflākī as} *Les saints des derviches tourneurs* (Paris, 1922), II, 10, n. 3.

20. "Oğuz etnolojisine dair tarihi notlar," pp. 209–11.

21. {Huart}, *Les saints des derviches tourneurs*, II, 10.

22. F. Chalandon, *Les Comnènes*. {*Études sur l'Empire Byzantin aux XI*[e] *et XII*[e] *siècles*} (Paris, 1900–13), II, 38.

23. Iorga, *Histoire de la vie byzantine*, III, 121.

24. Chalandon, op. cit., p. 500. {See H. Ahrweiler, "Les forteresses construites en Asie Mineure face à l'invasion seldjoucide," *Akten des XI. internationalen Byzantinistenkongresses, München, 1958* (Munich, 1960), pp. 182–89, and Clive Foss, "The defenses of Asia Minor against the Turks," *Greek Orthodox Theological Review*, 27 (1982), 145–205.}

25. Vasiliev, *Histoire de l'Empire Byzantin*, II, 282.

26. Wittek, *Das Fürstentum Mentesche*, p. 13.

27. {Togan, "Moğollar devrinde Anadolu'nun iktisadī vaziyeti,"} *THİTM*, 1 {1931}, 33.

28. {Now see Nicoara Beldiceanu, *Le timar dans l'état ottoman: début XIV*[e]*-début XVI*[e] *siècle* (Wiesbaden, 1980).}

29. {Byzantine subjects did not necessarily prefer Turkish rule. Many fled to Constantinople or the Aegean ports as is documented by Pachymeres, the correspondence of Patriarch Athanasius, and other thirteenth- and fourteenth-century sources.

Köprülü had in mind the incident from twelfth-century Anatolia, the islands in Lake Beyshehir, mentioned below. It must be kept in mind that Köprülü wrote on the eve of World War II when Jewish and other refugees were entering Turkey.}

30. Michael the Syrian, *Chronicle*, ed. and French trans. by J. B. Chabot {Paris, 1899–1910}, III, 222, 235, 390, 391; M. Brosset, *Deux historiens arméniens* (St. Petersburg, 1870–71), I {Cyriacus of Ganja}, 114; J. Laurent, "Sur les émirs danichmendites {jusqu'en 1104}," *Mélanges {offerts à M. Nicolas Iorga}* (Paris, 1933), p. 505; idem, *Byzance et les Turcs Seljoucides {dans l'Asie occidentale jusqu'en 1081}* (Paris, 1913–14), p. 74; idem, "Des Grecs aux Croisés. {Étude sur l'histoire d'Édesse entre 1071 et 1098}," *Byzantion*, 1 {1924}, 386; {J. T. Reinand, ed.}, *Géographie d'Aboulféda* {Paris, 1848}, I, xv. {Köprülü has a point, but many Armenian and Syriac sources used Muslim tolerance as a means of criticizing the Greek Orthodox Byzantines. The records of Greek Orthodox writers reveal that they had little freedom.}

31. Chalandon, *Les Comnènes*, II, 181.

32. "Autour de Digenis Akritas," *Byzantion*, 7 {1932}, 293.

33. {The Ottomans did have a policy of Islamization, although imposition was sporadic. See Anthony Bryer and Heath Lowry, eds., *Continuity and Change in late Byzantine and Early Ottoman Society* (Washington, D.C., 1986).}

34. {The claim that all the great statesmen of the fourteenth century were Turks is a pardonable lapse. The etymology of Evrenos cannot be taken seriously. This exaggeration reflects a defensive attitude that was common in Turkey after World War I.}

35. Thomsen, "Inscriptions de l'Orkhon déchiffrées," in *Mémoires de la Société Finno-Ugrienne*, (1896), {pp. 1–224}. See the index of Turkish words.

36. Al-Narshakhī, *Description {topographique et historique} de Boukhara*, ed. Ch. Schefer (Paris, 1892), p. 192.

37. Ibid., pp. 81, 82; Gardīzī, *Zain al-akhbār*, ed. Muḥammad Nāzim (Berlin, 1928), p. 48; Baihaqī, *The Ta'rīkh-i Baihaqī*, Bibliotheca Indica (Calcutta, 1862), p. 23.

38. Köprülüzāde, *Türkiye tarihi* (Istanbul, 1923), p. 82.

39. {On the whole question of the ghāzīs, see Wittek's "Deux chapitres." He took a completely different view from Köprülü (which Köprülü ignored in his later writings).}

40. *Turkestan Down to the Mongol Invasion* (London, 1928), p. 215.

41. Al-Ṭabarī, {*Ta'rīkh al-rusul wa 'l-mulūk*}, ed. M. J. de Goeje et al., {Leiden, 1879–1901}, series 3, II, 886.

42. *Riḥla*, ed. M. J. de Goeje (Leiden, 1907), p. 280. {English translation by R. J. C. Broadhurst as *The Travels of Ibn Jubayr* (London, 1952).}

43. R. Hartmann, "As-Sulamī's Risālat al-Malāmatīja," *Der Islam*, 8 (1918), {157–203}.

44. *Recueil de textes inédits concernant l'histoire de la mystique {en pays d'Islam}* (Paris, 1929), I, 69.

45. P. Kahle, "Die Futuwwa-Bündnisse des Kalifen en-Nāṣir (622–1225)," *Festschrift Georg Jacob*, {ed. Th. Menzel} (Leipzig, 1932), pp. 112–17; idem, "Ein Futuwwa-Erlass des Kalifen en-Nāṣir aus dem Jahre 604 (1207)," *Festschrift Max Freiherrn von Oppenheim*, {ed. E. F. Weidner} in *Archiv für Orientforschung* (Berlin, 1933), pp. 52–58.

46. Ibn Bībī, *Saljūqnāme*, Ayasofya Library {Istanbul}, MS. 2985. {See the facsimile edition of Ibn Bībī (Ankara, 1956), p. 155. This work was translated by H. W. Duda as *Die Seltschukengeschichte des Ibn Bībī* (Copenhagen, 1959). On futuwwa, see EI^2, s.v. "Futuwwa" (Cl. Cahen et al.).}

47. *Türk edebiyatında ilk mutasavvıflar*, p. 273.

48. For a bibliography, see the following two articles by F. Taeschner: "Futuwwa-Studien, die Futuwwabünde in der Türkei und ihre Literatur," *Islamica*, 5 (1932), {285–333}, and "Die islamischen Futuwwabünde," *ZDMG*, N.F. 12 (87, 1933), {6–49}.

49. {Köprülü is unfair to ʿĀshıq Pasha-Zāde. Cf. Ménage, "The Beginnings of Ottoman Historiography," pp. 174–75. It should be mentioned that no one today equates ghāzīs with akhīs.}

50. P. Wittek, "Zur Geschichte Angoras im Mittelalter," *Festschrift Georg Jacob*, {ed. Th. Menzel (Leipzig, 1932)}, p. 349.

51. *Türk edebiyatında ilk mutasavvıflar*, p. 241.

52. Massignon, {*La passion d'al-Hosayn ibn Mansour*} *al-Hallāj, martyr mystique de l'Islam*, (Paris, 1914–22), I, 399; idem, *EI*[1], s.v. "Ṣinf."

53. "Georgios Gemistos Plethon. {Ein Beitrag zur Frage der Übertragung von islamischen Geistesgut nach dem Abendlande,"} *Der Islam*, 18 (1929), 236–43. {This idea never found convincing proof or substantial support among Byzantinists.}

54. Vasiliev, *Histoire de l'Empire Byzantin*, II, 328–29.

55. Taeschner, "Futuwwa-Studien," pp. 294–95.

56. *Le voyage d'outremer*, pp. 82, 118.

57. {Now see Mikail Bayram, *Bacıyan-ı Rum: Selçuklular zamanında genç kız teşkilatı* (Konya, 1987).}

58. Köprülüzāde, "Influence du chamanisme turco-mongol sur les ordres mystiques musulmans," {*Mémoires de l'Institut de Turcologie de l'Université de Stanboul*, new series, I} (Istanbul, 1929), p. 12 {summary in *Actes V*[e] *Congrès International d'Histoire des Religions* (1929), pp. 279–82}.

59. "Abū Isḥāq Kāzerūnī und die Isḥāquī-Derwische in Anatolien," *Der Islam*, 19 (1931), 18–26.

60. W. Caskel, {a note to Köprülü's aforesaid article}, *Der Islam*, 19 {1931}, 284–85.

61. *Le voyage d'outremer*, p. 131.

62. *Türk edebiyatında ilk mutasavvıflar*, pp. 31–201.

63. Köprülüzāde, "Anadolu'da islāmiyet," offprint, pp. 50–56.

64. Ibid., pp. 54–55.

65. "Les origines du Bektachisme."

66. {"Zur Stifterlegende der Bektaschis,"} *Orientalische Literaturzeitung*, 31 (1928), col. 1038–57.

67. {Now securely dated 1302. There is no proof that the battle that Ottoman sources give as Koyunhisarı was the same as that at Baphaeum (Bapheus). See İnalcık, "The Rise of Ottoman Historiography," in Lewis and Holt, eds., *Historians of the Middle East*, pp. 152–53.}

68. {The Thracian campaigns did not take place under Ottoman suzerainty. See Beldiceanu-Steinherr, "La conquête d'Andrinople."}

69. {The principle of "indivisibility of sovereignty" did not operate in early Ottoman history. Cf. Joseph Fletcher, "The Turco-Mongolian Monarchic Tradition in the Ottoman Empire," *Harvard Ukranian Studies*, 3–4 (1979–80), 236–251.}

70. {The Balkan religious situation was actually more complicated. See John V. A. Fine, Jr., *The Bosnian Church* (New York, 1975).}

71. "Bizans müesseselerinin osmanlı müesseseleri üzerine te'siri," pp. 165–313. A short summary of the conclusions reached in this work was published in French as "Les institutions byzantines ont-elles joué un rôle dans la formation des institutions ottomanes?" in *VIIe Congrès International des Sciences Historiques, résumés des communications présentées au congrès* (Warsaw, 1933), I, 297–302. Believing that he had understood my thesis after quickly reading this summary, R. Guilland was able to write that I had "resolved the question of Byzantine influence in the negative, but, it seems, without the impartiality or serenity befitting an historian," "Institutions byzantines, institutions musulmans?" in *Annales d'Histoire Économique et Sociale*, 6 (1934), 426. I stated in my original work that there was positive evidence of Byzantine influence on Muslim institutions, especially in the Umayyad and ʿAbbāsid periods. As for the Turks, I believe that I showed that they were under this influence before and not after the establishment of the Ottoman state. As for equating Islamic institutions with Ottoman institutions, I will naturally leave the responsibility for that to Mr. Guilland. {It should be repeated that Köprülü had no access to Byzantine sources. Cf. Vryonis, "The Byzantine Legacy and Ottoman Forms," *DOP*, 23–24 (1969–70), 251–308.}

GLOSSARY

Abdāl	Name sometimes given to itinerant dervishes
Akhī	Member of a religious fraternity
Alp	Hero, march warrior
ʿAyyār	"Vagrant," "rabble," an unemployed person associated with the *futuwwa*
Bābā	"Father," honorific title used especially in dervish circles
Bey	Title of a prince, ruler, chief
Beylik	Principality, region ruled by a *bey*
Devshirme	Levy of Christian boys who were converted to Islam and trained for posts in military or administrative service
Dīwān	Government ministry or governing council
Emīr	Military commander
Emīr ül-ümerā	Commander-in-chief
Futuwwa	A semi-religious fraternity with special code of behavior, often associated with guilds
Ghāzī	Warrior for the faith
Iqṭāʿ	Grant of state lands or revenue by a ruler in exchange for service, usually military
Jizya	Head tax on non-Muslims
Kānūnnāme	Digest of sultanic laws

Khān	Title usually used for subordinate rulers, not to be confused with the same word meaning inn or warehouse
Khāṣṣ	Part of the royal domain
Madrasa	Islamic college of law
Mahdī	Restorer, messiah
Mürid	*Ṣūfī* disciple
Shaikh	*Ṣūfī* master, elder
Sipāhī	Cavalryman
Ṣūfī	Muslim mystic, mystical
Tekke	Dervish lodge
Timar	An allotment, for a period of years, of a portion of revenue from land
Waqf	Pious endowment

BIBLIOGRAPHY

Note: Turkish works published before 1929 are in the Arabic script. Works in braces were added to the notes by the translator.

Abdülkadir. " 'Orun' ve 'ülüş' meselesi" [The question of '*orun*' and '*ülüş*']. *THİTM*, 1 (1931), 121–33.

Aflākī. *Les saints des derviches tourneurs*. French trans. Cl. Huart. 2 vols. Paris, 1922.

{Ahmedī. *Iskendernāme*. Istanbul, 1947 and 1988.}

{Ahrweiler, H. "Les forteresses construites en Asie Mineure face à l'invasion seldjoucide" in *Akten des XI. internationalen Byzantinistenkongresses, München, 1958* (Munich, 1960), pp. 182–89.}

{Akın, Himmet. *Aydın oğulları tarihi hakkında bir araştırma* [Research on the history of the Aydınids]. 2nd ed. Ankara, 1968.}

Anonymous. Ed. "Osmānī kānūnnāmeleri" [Ottoman *kānūnnāmes.*] *MTM*, (1331), nr. 1, 49–112, nr. 2, 303–48.

Anonymous. *Saljūqnāme*. Bibliothèque Nationale, Persian supplement, MS 1559. {Published in facsimile and translated by Feridun Uzluk as *Tarih-i āl-i Selçuk (Selçuknāme) der Anadolu: Anadolu Selçukluları devleti tarihi* [The *Tarih-i āl-i Selçuk (Selçuknāme)* of Anatolia: the history of the Seljuk state of Anatolia]. Ankara, 1952.}

{Al-Aqsarāyī. *Musāmarat al-akhbār*. Ed. Osman Turan. Ankara, 1944. Turkish trans. M. Nuri Gençosman. *Selçuklu devletleri tarihi* [The history of the Seljuk states]. Ankara, 1943. Summary German trans. Fikret Işıltan. *Die Seltschuken Geschichte des Akserayī*. Leipzig, 1943.}

Ārif, Mehmed. Ed. "Kānūnnāme-i āl-i Osmān." *Kānūnnāmes* of Mehmed II and Süleymān the Magnificent published as separate supplements to *TOEM*, (1328 and 1329), nrs. 13–19.

{Artuk, İbrahim and Cevriye. *İstanbul arkeoloji müzeleri teşhirdeki islami sikkeler kataloğu* [Catalogue of the Islamic coins on exhibit in the Istanbul archeological museums]. 2 vols. Istanbul, 1970–74.}

Astarābādī, ʿAzīz b. Ardashīr. *Bazm u razm* (or *Manāqib-i Qāḍī Burhān al-Dīn*). Istanbul, 1928.

Babinger, F. "Der Islam in Kleinasien. Neue Wege der Islamforschung." *ZDMG*, N.F., 76 (1922), 126–52.

———*Die Geschichtsschreiber der Osmanen und ihre Werke*. Leipzig, 1927.

de Backer, L. *Guillaume de Rubrouck*. Paris, 1877.

Baihaqī. *The Ta'rīkh-i Baihaqī* (or *Ta'rīkh-i Masʿūdī*). Bibliotheca Indica, Calcutta, 1862.

Bang, W. and J. Marquart. *Osttürkische Dialektstudien*. Berlin, 1914.

Bāqī. *Faḍā'il al-jihād*. MS, no location given.

{Barkan, Ö. L. *XV. ve XVI. asırlarda osmanlı imparatorluğunda ziraī ekonominin hukukī ve malī esasları* [The juridical and financial bases of the rural economy in the Ottoman Empire in the fifteenth and sixteenth centuries]. Istanbul, 1943.}

Barthold, W. "Ḳāyı̄," *EI*[1].

———{Unidentified article.} *Zapiski Vostochnago Otdyeleniya Imperatorskago Russkago Arkheologicheskago Obshchestva*, vol. 18, pp. 124–37.

———*Turkestan down to the Mongol Invasion*. London, 1928.

{Beldiceanu, Nicoara. *Le timar dans l'état ottoman: début XIV*ᵉ*-début XVI*ᵉ *siècle*. Wiesbaden, 1980.}

{Beldiceanu-Steinherr, Irène. "La conquête d'Andrinople par les Turcs: la pénétration turque en Thrace et la valeur des chroniques ottomanes." *Traveaux et Mémoires, Centre de Recherche d'Histoire et Civilization Byzantines*, 1 (1965), 439–61.}

———{"Fiscalité et formes de possession de la terre arable dans l'Anatolie pré-ottomane." *JESHO*, 19 (1976), 233–322.}

Bertrandon de la Broquière. *Le voyage d'outremer*. Ed. Ch. Schefer. Paris, 1892.

Blochet, E. "Le pays de Tchata et les Ephtalites." *Atti della Reale Accademia dei Lincei. Rendiconti*, 6th series, 1 (1925), 331–51.

Bouvat, L. "Les premiers mystiques dans la littérature turque." *Revue de Monde Musulman*, 43 (1921), 236–82.

Bratianu, G. I. *Recherches sur le commerce génois dans la Mer Noir au XIIIe siècle*. Paris, 1929.

{Bayram, Mikail. *Bacıyan-ı Rum: Selçuklular zamanında genç kız teşkilatı* [*Bājiyān-ı rūm*: an organization of young women at the time of the Seljuks]. Konya, 1987.}

Brockelmann, C. "Alttürkestanische Volkspoesie I." *Asia Major*, 1 (1923), 3–24, 2 (1924), 24–44.

———*Das Nationalgefül der Türken im Licht der Geschichte*. Halle, 1918.

Brosset, M. *Deux historiens arméniens*. 2 vols. St. Petersburg, 1870–71.

{Bryer, Anthony. *The Empire of Trebizond and the Pontos*. London, 1980.}

{Bryer, Anthony and Heath Lowry. Eds. *Continuity and Change in late Byzantine and Early Ottoman Society*. Washington, D.C., 1986.}

{Bryer, Anthony and Davie Winfield. *The Byzantine Monuments and Topography of the Pontos*. 2 vols. Washington, D. C., 1985.}

{Cahen, Claude. "La première pénétration turque en Asie-Mineure." Reprinted in his *Turcobyzantina et Oriens Christianus*. London, 1974. Article I, 5–67.}

———{"Ibn Saʿīd sur l'Asie Mineure seldjuqide" in *Turcobyzantina*. Article XI, 41–50.}

———{*Pre-Ottoman Turkey*. New York, 1968.}

———{*La Turquie pré-ottomane*. Istanbul, 1988.}

{Cahen, Claude, et al. "Futuwwa," *EI*[2].}

{Cantacuzenus, John. *Geschichte / Johannes Kantakuzenus*. German trans. Georgios Fatouros and Tilman Krischer. 2 vols. Stuttgart, 1982–86.}

Caskel, W. A note to Köprülü's article on Abū Isḥāq Kāzerūnī. *Der Islam*, 19 (1931), 284–85.

Chalandon, F. *Les Comnènes. Études sur l'Empire Byzantin aux XIe et XIIe siècles*. 2 vols. Paris, 1900–13.

Charignon, A. *Le livre de Marco Polo*. 3 vols. Pekin, 1924.

{Combe, Ét., et al. *Répertoire chronologique d'épigraphie arabe*. 16 vols. Cairo, 1931–64. Index, Cairo, 1975.}

Corbin, H. "Pour l'anthropologie philosophique: un traité persan inédit de Suhrawardī d'Alep." *Recherches Philosophiques*, 2 (1932–33), 371–423.

{Darrouzès, Jean. *Les régestes de 1310 à 1376*, fasc. 5, vol. 1 of *Les régestes des actes du patriarcat de Constantinople*. Paris, 1977.}

{Dawson, Christopher. Trans. *The Mongol Mission: Narratives and Letters of the Franciscan Missionaries in Mongolia and China in the Thirteenth and Fourteenth Centuries*. New York, 1955.}

Diehl, Ch. *Byzance: grandeur et décadence*. Paris, 1919.

———*La société byzantine à l'époque des Comnènes*. Paris, 1929.

Evliyā Chelebī. *Seyāḥatnāme*. Istanbul, 1314–18 (vols. 1–6), 1928 (vols. 7–8), 1935 (vol. 9), 1938 (vol. 10).

{Fine, Jr., John V. A. *The Bosnian Church*. New York, 1975.}

{Flemming, Barbara. *Landschaaftsgeschichte von Pamphylien, Pisidien und Lykien im Spätmittelalter*. Wiesbaden, 1964.}

{Fletcher, Joseph. "The Turco-Mongolian Monarchic Tradition in the Ottoman Empire." *Harvard Ukranian Studies*, 3–4 (1979–80), 236–251.}

{Foss, Clive. "The defenses of Asia Minor against the Turks." *Greek Orthodox Theological Review*, 27 (1982), 145–205.}

Frazer, J. G. *Le rameau d'or*. Paris, 1924. {Originally in English as *The Golden Bough*. Recent edition, New York, 1942.}

Gardīzī. *Zain al-akhbār*. Ed. Muḥammad Nāzim. Berlin, 1928.

{Garsoian, Nina. *The Paulician Heresy*. The Hague, 1967.}

Gibbons, H. A. *The Foundation of the Ottoman Empire*. Oxford, 1916.

Giese, F. "Das Problem der Entstehung des osmanischen Reich."

Zeitschrift für Semitistik und verwandte Gebeit, 2 (1924), 246–71.

{Giesecke, Heinz. *Das Werk des ʿAzīz ibn Ardaşīr Astarābādī, eine Quelle zur Geschichte des Spätmittelalters in Kleinasien*. Leipzig, 1940.}

{Gregoras, Nicephorus. *Rhomaische Geschichte = Historia Rhomaike [von] Nikephoros Gregoras*. German trans. Jan Louis van Dieten. 3 vols. Stuttgart, 1973–88.}

Grégoire, H. "Autour de Digenis Akritas." *Byzantion*, 7 (1932), 287–302.

Grousset, René. *Histoire de l'Asie*. 3 vols. Paris, 1921–22.

Guilland, R. "Institutions byzantines, institutions musulmans?" *Annales d'Histoire Economique et Sociale*, 6 (1934), 426–27.

Guyard, S. *Géographie d'Aboulféda*. Vol. II, pt. 2. Paris, 1883.

Ḥamd Allāh Mustawfī Qazvīnī. *Ta'rīkh-i Guzīda*. 2 vols. London, 1910–13.

Hartmann, R. "As-Sulamī's Risālat al-malāmatīja." *Der Islam*, 8 (1918), 157–203.

Hasluck, F. W. *Christianity and Islam under the Sultans*. 2 vols. Oxford, 1929.

{Hendy, Michael. *Studies in the Byzantine Monetary Economy*. Cambridge, 1985.}

———{*The Economy, Fiscal Administration and Coinage of Byzantium*. Northampton, 1989.}

{Hennequin, Gilles. *Catalogue des monnaies musulmanes de la Bibliothèque Nationale*. Vol. 5, *Asie pré-mongole: les Salğuqs et leur successeurs*. Paris, 1985.}

Heyd, W. *Histoire du commerce du Levant au moyen-âge*. 2 vols. Paris, 1923.

{Hourani, A. H. and S. M. Stern. Eds. *The Islamic City*. Oxford, 1970.}

Houtsma, Th. "Over de Geschiedenis der Seldjuken van Klein-Azie." *Verslagen en Mededeelingen d. k. Akad. v. Wetensch. Afd. letterkunde*. 3rd series, pt. 9. Amsterdam, 1893, pp. 133–53.

Huart, Cl. "De la valeur historique des mémoirs des derviches tourneurs." *JA*, 11th series, 19 (1922), 308–17.

———"Les anciens derviches turcs." *Journal des Savants*, 20 (1922), 5–18.

———Review of Gibbons, *The Foundation of the Ottoman Empire*. *JA*, 11th series, 9 (1917), 345–50.

———Review of Gibbons, *The Foundation of the Ottoman Empire*. *Journal des Savants*, April, 1917, pp. 157–66.

Ibn al-ʿAdīm, Kamāl al-Dīn. *Histoire d'Alep*. French trans. E. Blochet. Paris, 1900.

Ibn Bībī. *Saljūqnāme*. Ayasofya Library, Istanbul, MS. 2985. {Facsimile ed. Ankara, 1956. German trans. H. W. Duda. *Die Seltschukengeschichte des Ibn Bībī*. Copenhagen, 1959.}

Ibn Jubayr. *Riḥla*. Ed. M. J. de Goeje. Leiden, 1907. {English trans. R. J. C. Broadhurst. *The Travels of Ibn Jubayr*. London, 1952.}

{İnalcık, Halil. "The Rise of Ottoman Historiography." *Historians of the Middle East*. Eds. Bernard Lewis and Peter Holt. Oxford, 1962, pp. 152–67.}

———{"Ḳānūn," *EI*[2].}

Iorga, N. *Histoire de la vie byzantine. Empire et civilization*. 3 vols. Bucharest, 1934.

Jūzjānī. *Ṭabaqāt-i Nāṣirī*. Persian text, Calcutta, 1864.

Kahle, P. "Die Futuwwa-Bündnisse des Kalifen en-Nāṣir (622–1225)." *Festschrift Georg Jacob*. Ed. Th. Menzel. Leipzig, 1932, pp. 112–27.

———"Ein Futuwwa-Erlass des Kalifen en-Nāṣir aus dem Jahr 604 (1207)." *Festschrift Max Freiherrn von Oppenheim*. Ed. E. F. Weidner in *Archiv für Orientforschung*. Berlin, 1933, pp. 52–58.

Köprülü (zāde), M. Fuad. "Turkmens" (Literature), *EI*[1].

———"Türk edebiyat tarihinde usul" [Method in the history of Turkish literature]. *Bilgi Mecmuası*, 1 (1329/1913), 3–52.

———"Türk edebiyatında āşık tarzı'nın menşe ve tekāmülü hakkında bir tecrübe [An essay on the origin and development of the *āshıq* form in Turkish literature]. *MTM*, (1331), nr. 1, 5–46.

———"Selçukīler zamanında Anadolu'da Türk medeniyeti" [Turkish civilization in Anatolia at the time of the Seljuks]. *MTM*, (1331), nr. 5, 193–232.

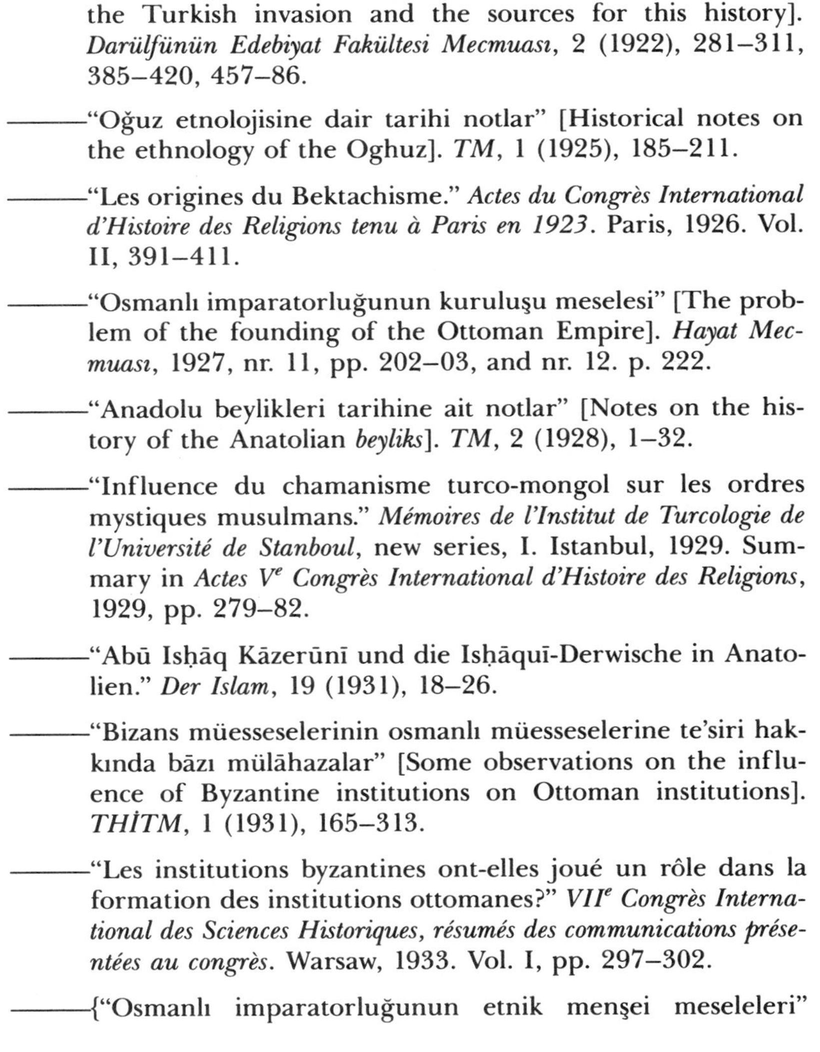

———"Anadolu'da islāmiyet: Türk istilāsından sonra Anadolu tarih-i dinisine bir nazar ve bu tarihin menbaları" [Islam in Anatolia: A review of the religious history of Anatolia after the Turkish invasion and the sources for this history]. *Darülfünün Edebiyat Fakültesi Mecmuası*, 2 (1922), 281–311, 385–420, 457–86.

———"Oğuz etnolojisine dair tarihi notlar" [Historical notes on the ethnology of the Oghuz]. *TM*, 1 (1925), 185–211.

———"Les origines du Bektachisme." *Actes du Congrès International d'Histoire des Religions tenu à Paris en 1923*. Paris, 1926. Vol. II, 391–411.

———"Osmanlı imparatorluğunun kuruluşu meselesi" [The problem of the founding of the Ottoman Empire]. *Hayat Mecmuası*, 1927, nr. 11, pp. 202–03, and nr. 12. p. 222.

———"Anadolu beylikleri tarihine ait notlar" [Notes on the history of the Anatolian *beyliks*]. *TM*, 2 (1928), 1–32.

———"Influence du chamanisme turco-mongol sur les ordres mystiques musulmans." *Mémoires de l'Institut de Turcologie de l'Université de Stanboul*, new series, I. Istanbul, 1929. Summary in *Actes Ve Congrès International d'Histoire des Religions*, 1929, pp. 279–82.

———"Abū Isḥāq Kāzerūnī und die Isḥāquī-Derwische in Anatolien." *Der Islam*, 19 (1931), 18–26.

———"Bizans müesseselerinin osmanlı müesseselerine te'siri hakkında bāzı mülāhazalar" [Some observations on the influence of Byzantine institutions on Ottoman institutions]. *THİTM*, 1 (1931), 165–313.

———"Les institutions byzantines ont-elles joué un rôle dans la formation des institutions ottomanes?" *VIIe Congrès International des Sciences Historiques, résumés des communications présentées au congrès*. Warsaw, 1933. Vol. I, pp. 297–302.

———{"Osmanlı imparatorluğunun etnik menşei meseleleri"

[Problems of the ethnic origin of the Ottoman Empire]. *Belleten*, 7 (1943), 219–313.}

———{"Kay kabilesi hakkında yeni notlar" [New notes on the Qay tribe]. *Belleten*, 8 (1944), 421–52.}

———*Türk edebiyatında ilk mutasavvıflar* [Early mystics in Turkish literature]. Istanbul, 1918. {2nd revised ed., 1966; rpt. Ankara, 1981.}

———*Türkiye tarihi* [The history of Turkey]. Istanbul, 1923.

———*Türk edebiyatı tarihi* [The history of Turkish literature]. Istanbul, 1926.

Kraelitz, Fr. "Ḳānūnnāme Sultan Meḥmeds des Eroberers." *MOG*, 1 (1921–22), 13–48.

Kramers, J. H. "Wer war Osman?" *Acta Orientalia*, 6 (1928), 242–54.

———"Türks," pt. IV, "History," *EI*[1].

Langer, W. L., and R. P. Blake. "The Rise of the Ottoman Turks and its Historical Background." *American Historical Review*, 37 (1931–32), 488–505.

Laurent, J. "Des Grecs aux Croisés. Étude sur l'histoire d'Édesse entre 1071 et 1098." *Byzantion*, 1 (1924), 367–449.

———"Sur les émirs danichmendites jusqu'en 1104." *Mélanges offerts à M. Nicolas Iorga*. Paris, 1933, pp. 499–506.

———*Byzance et les Turcs Seljoucides dans l'Asie occidentale jusqu'en 1081*. Paris, 1913–14.

Lavisse, E. and A. Rambaud. *Histoire générale de IVe siècle à nos jour*. 12 vols. Paris, 1893–1901.

de Mas Latrie, L. *L'île de Chypre, sa situation présente et ses souvenirs du moyen-âge*. Paris, 1879.

{Lemerle, Paul. *L'emirat d'Aydın, Byzance et l'Occident*. Paris, 1957.}

{Lindner, Rudi. *Nomads and Ottomans in Medieval Anatolia*. Bloomington, Indiana, 1983.}

Massignon, L. "Ṣinf," *EI*[1].

———*La passion d'al-Hosayn ibn Mansour al-Hallāj, martyr mystique de l'Islam*. 2 vols. Paris, 1914–22.

———*Recueil de textes inédits concernant l'histoire de la mystique en pays d'Islam*. Paris, 1929.

{Mélikoff, Irene. *Le destan d'Umur Pacha*. Paris, 1954.}

———{*La geste de Melik Danişmend*. Paris, 1960.}

{Ménage, V. L. "The Beginnings of Ottoman Historiography." *Historians of the Middle East*. Eds. Bernard Lewis and Peter Holt. Oxford, 1962, pp. 168–79.}

———{"The *Menāqib* of Yakhshi Faqīh." *BSOAS*, 26 (1963), 50–54.}

———{"On the Recensions of Uruj's 'History of the Ottomans.' " *BSOAS*, 30 (1967), 314–22.}

———{"Bihis͟htī," *EI*[2].}

———{"Kemāl Pas͟ha-Zāde," *EI*[2].}

Menzel, Th. "Köprülüzāde Mehmed Fuād's Werke über die ersten mystiker in der türkischen Literature." *KCA*, 2 (1932), 281–310, 345–57, 406–22.

Michael the Syrian. *Chronicle*. Ed. and trans. J. B. Chabot. 2 vols. Paris, 1899–1910.

{Millī Kütüphane Genel Müdürlüğü. *Selçuklu tarihi, Alparslan ve Malazgirt bibliografyası* [Bibliography of Seljuk history, Alparslan and Malazgird]. Ankara, 1971.}

Mükrimin Halil Yınanç. *Düstūrnāme-i Enverī*. 2 vols. Istanbul, 1928–30.

Müneccim-başı. *Jāmi*ʿ *al-duwal*. See Babinger, *Die Geschichtsschreiber der Osmanen und ihre Werke*, nr. 205.

Al-Narshakhī. *Description topographique et historique de Boukhara*. Ed. Ch. Schefer. Paris, 1892.

Németh, J. Review of A. Fischer, *Die Vokalharmonie Endungen an den Fremdwörtern des Türkischen*. *ZDMG*, nr. 75 (1921), 275–78.

Nöldeke, Th. "Auszüge aus Neśrī's Geschichte des osmanischen Hauses." *ZDMG*, 13 (1859), 176–218, 15 (1861), 333–380.

{Ocak, Ahmet Yaşar. *La revolte de Baba Resul*. Ankara, 1989.}

Omont, H. "Notice du MS. Nov. Acq. Franç. 10.050 de la Bibliothèque Nationale contenant un nouveau texte français de 'La fleur des histoires de la terre d'orient' de Haython." *Notices et Extraits des Manuscrits de la Bibliothèque Nationale et Autres Bibliothèques*, 38 (1903), 237–92.

{Özdemir, Hasan. *Die altosmanischen Chroniken als Quelle zur türkischen Volkskunde*. Freiburg, 1975.}

{Pachymeres, George. *Relations historiques / Georges Pachymeres*. French trans. Vitalien Laurent and Albert Failler. 2 vols. Paris, 1984.}

Pauthier, G. *Le Livre de Marco Polo*. 2 vols. Paris, 1865.

Pelliot, P. "À propos des Comans." *JA*, 11th series, 15 (1920), 125–85.

{Phillipides-Braat, Anna. "La captivité de Palamas chez les Turcs: dossier et commentaire." *Travaux et Mémoirs, Centre de Recherche d'Histoire et Civilization Byzantines*, 7 (1979), 109–22.}

Pirenne, H. *Les villes du moyen-âge*. Brussels, 1927. {English trans. *Medieval Cities*. Princeton, New Jersey, 1925.}

Quatremère, É. *Histoire des Mongols de la Perse*. Paris, 1836.

Rashīd al-Dīn. *Jāmiᶜ al-tawārīkh*. On this work, see J. A. Boyle, *The Successors of Genghis Khan* (New York, 1971).

Recueil des historiens des Croisades: Documents arméniens. 2 vols. Paris, 1869–1906.

Recueil des historiens des Croisades: Historiens orientaux. 5 vols. Paris, 1872–1906.

Reinaud, J. T. *Géographie d'Aboulféda*. Vol. 1, and vol. 2, pt. 1. Paris, 1848.

{Remler, Philip. "Ottoman, Isfendiyarid, and Eretnid Coinage: A Currency Community in Fourteenth-Century Anatolia." *American Numismatic Society Museum Notes*, 25 (1980), 167–88.}

{Savvides, Alexios G. C. *Byzantium in the Near East*. Thessalonike, 1981.}

Schaeder, H. "Zur Stifterlegende der Bektaschis." *Orientalische Literaturzeitung*, 3 (1928), col. 1038–57.

Schefer, Ch. Ed. *Recueil de textes et de traductions*. Paris, 1889.

{Schreiner, Peter. Ed. and trans. *Die byzantinischen Kleinchroniken*. 3 vols. Vienna, 1975–79.}

Sharaf al-Dīn ʿAlī Yazdī. *Zafernāme*. Bibliotheca Indica, 2 vols. Calcutta, 1887–88.

Shikārī. *Vekāyiʿ-nāmeleri*. See above, ch. 1, nt. 31.

Skok, P. "Restes de la langue turque dans les Balkans." *Revue International des Études Balkaniques*, 1 (1935), 247–60.

{Smith, Jr., John Masson. "Mongol manpower and Persian population." *JESHO*, 18 (1975), 271–99.}

{Sümer, Faruk. "Anadolu'ya yalnız göçebe Türkler mi geldi?" [Did only nomadic Turks come to Anatolia?]. *Belleten*, 24 (1960), 567–94.}

———{*Yaban Pazarı: An Important International Fair in the Saljuq Period*. Istanbul, 1985.}

Al-Ṭabarī. *Taʾrīkh al-rusul wa ʾl-mulūk*. Ed. M. J. de Goeje et al. 15 vols. Leiden, 1879–1901.

Taeschner, F. "Georgios Gemistos Plethon. Ein Beitrag zur Frage der Übertragung von islamischen Geistesgut nach dem Abendlande." *Der Islam*, 18 (1929), 236–43.

———"Futuwwa-Studien, die Futuwwabünde in der Türkei und ihre Literatur." *Islamica*, 5 (1932), 285–333.

———"Die islamischen Futuwwabünde." *ZDMG*, N.F., 12 (87, 1933), 6–49.

Thomsen, V. "Inscriptions de l'Orkhon déchiffrées." *Mémoires de la Société Finno-Ugrienne*, 5 (1896), 1–224.

Togan, Zeki Validi. "Moğollar devrinde Anadolu'nun iktisadī vaziyeti [Economic conditions in Anatolia in the Mongol period]. *THİTM*, 1 (1931), 1–42.

———{*Oğuz destani* [The Oghuz epic]. Istanbul, 1972.}

Tschudi, Rudolf. *Von alten osmanischen Reich*. Tübingen, 1930.

{Turan, Osman. *Selçuklular zamanında Türkiye tarihi* [The history of Turkey in the Seljuk period]. Istanbul, 1971.}

Uzunçarşılı, İsmail Hakkı. *Kütahya Şehri* [The city of Kütahya]. Istanbul, 1932.

{Varlık, Mustafa Çetin. *Germiyan-oğulları tarihi, 1300–1429* [The history of the Germiyānids, 1300–1429]. Ankara, 1974.}

Vasiliev, A. A. *Histoire de l'Empire Byzantin*. 2 vols. Paris, 1932.

{Vryonis, Speros. "The Byzantine Legacy and Ottoman Forms." *DOP*, 23–24 (1969–70), 251–308.}

———{*The Decline of Medieval Hellenism in Asia Minor*. Berkeley, California, 1971.}

Wittek, P. "Zur Geschichte Angoras im Mittelalter." *Festschrift Georg Jacob*. Ed. Th. Menzel. Leipzig, 1932, pp. 329–54.

———{"Der Stammbaum der Osmanen." *Der Islam*, 14, (1925), 94–100.}

———{"Deux chapitres de l'histoire des Turcs de Roum." *Byzantion*, 11 (1936), 285–319.}

———{"Yazijioghlu ʿAli on the Christian Turks of the Dobruja." *BSOAS*, 14 (1952), 639–68.}

———*Das Fürstentum Mentesche*. Istanbul, 1934.

———*The Rise of the Ottoman Empire*. London, 1938.

{Yücel, Yaşar. *Kadı Burhaneddin Ahmed ve devleti (1344–1398)* [Qāḍī Burhān al-Dīn Aḥmad and his state (1344–1398)]. Ankara, 1970.}

———{*Çoban-oğulları, Candar-oğulları beylikleri* [The *beyliks* of the Chobanids and Jāndārids]. Ankara, 1980.}

{Yule, Henry and Henri Cordier. Eds. *The Book of Ser Marco Polo*. 3rd ed. London, 1921.}

{Zachariadou, Elizavet. *Romania and the Turks*. London, 1985.}

INDEX